"*The Vanishing Evangelical* is not only a fitting epitaph of Calvin Miller's well-lived life but also a prophetic trumpet blast to the church given to us as he entered eternity. Upon reading his visionary summons, I was duly convicted, then encouraged; challenged, then affirmed; guilty as charged, then exonerated with grace. Calvin Miller's amazingly insightful work is written for such a time as this, calling a sedated church back to her first love and to her rightful place."

Wayne Cordeiro, founder and senior pastor
of New Hope Christian Fellowship, Honolulu, Hawaii

"Calvin Miller was a pastor, professor, artist, apologist, evangelist, and writer of renown. He was also my friend, colleague, racquetball mate, and discussion partner. This is the last book he wrote, and it's well worth the read. I wish Calvin were still here so that I could take him to Starbucks to chat about several things he wrote in this volume, but I'm sure he is occupied with higher things in a better place. We are still tracking with you, Calvin!"

Timothy George, founding dean
of Beeson Divinity School of Samford University;
general editor of the *Reformation Commentary on Scripture*

"Calvin Miller knew the evangelical world from many perspectives—as a pastor, church planter, bestselling author, and teacher. In *The Vanishing Evangelical*, he summons his decades of experience and his considerable talents to craft a powerful indictment of the current state of the evangelical church. Dealing with challenges such as a declining interest in worship and discipleship, postmodern thought, wavering orthodoxy, and more, the book nevertheless points to factors that indicate the potential for a more promising future. Church leaders should take seriously both Miller's concerns and his prescriptions for the future of the church."

Michael Duduit, executive editor of *Preaching* magazine;
dean of the College of Christian Studies
at Anderson University, Anderson, South Carolina

"Calvin Miller's crowning work sizzles with prophetic zeal. Like Jesus, Miller had a passion that increased as his life on this planet ebbed. That passion comes through in the pages of this book."

David Murrow, author of *Why Men Hate Going to Church*

THE

VANISHING

EVANGELICAL

THE
VANISHING
EVANGELICAL

SAVING THE CHURCH FROM ITS OWN SUCCESS
BY RESTORING WHAT **REALLY MATTERS**

CALVIN MILLER

BakerBooks
a division of Baker Publishing Group
Grand Rapids, Michigan

© 2013 by Calvin Miller

Published by Baker Books
a division of Baker Publishing Group
P.O. Box 6287, Grand Rapids, MI 49516-6287
www.bakerbooks.com

Printed in the United States of America

Library of Congress Cataloging-in-Publication Data is on file at the Library of Congress, Washington, DC.

ISBN 978-0-8010-1551-9

Unless otherwise indicated, Scripture quotations are from the Holy Bible, New International Version®. NIV®. Copyright © 1973, 1978, 1984, 2011 by Biblica, Inc.™ Used by permission of Zondervan. All rights reserved worldwide. www.zondervan.com

Scripture marked KJV is taken from the King James Version.

Scripture marked Message is taken from *The Message* by Eugene H. Peterson, copyright © 1993, 1994, 1995, 2000, 2001, 2002. Used by permission of NavPress Publishing Group. All rights reserved.

Scripture marked NKJV is taken from the New King James Version. Copyright © 1982 by Thomas Nelson, Inc. Used by permission. All rights reserved.

The author is represented by WordServe Literary Group.

13 14 15 16 17 · 18 19   7 6 5 4 3 2 1

Contents

Contents

Preface

I want to deal with only two questions as I begin this book. The first is an issue of basic definitions as I try to answer the question: Who are evangelicals? The second question is: Who are my sources?

Who Are Evangelicals?

At the outset of our time together in the following pages, I want to spend a few paragraphs on this most basic definition. I do it because almost everyone who is an evangelical uses the term with a bit of pride and confidence, but almost no two of them have exactly the same definition. A most casual but none-too-defining definition is this one from Got Questions Ministries:

> Evangelicalism is a somewhat broad term used to describe a movement within Protestantism that is characterized by an emphasis on having a personal relationship with Jesus Christ. This relationship begins when a person receives Christ's forgiveness and is spiritually reborn. Those who ascribe to this belief are called evangelicals.[1]

This is a most minimal definition, and even so is not totally correct since many who are *born again* do not consider themselves *evangelicals*.

Being an evangelical is really a kind of mystique bound up in conservative theology. The term seems to exist on two levels. On the *mystique* level it suggests a whole set of attitudes and faith practices that are not bound up in traditional church covenants or doctrines. The word is also *activistic*. Those who call themselves evangelicals tend to hold to traditional views of morality, creation, and miracles as well as the view of God in history. Further, evangelicals tend to believe in the consummation of the ages with at least some of its biblical and apocalyptic imagery.

On the other hand, it generally carries with it a doctrinal subbase that grew out of American fundamentalism in the early to midyears of the nineteenth century. For further reading on this subject, I recommend George Marsden's book *Reforming Fundamentalism*.[2] In 1948 during the formation of the *new evangelicalism*, as it came to be called in the late 1950s, Carl F. H. Henry said, "Evangelical Christianity is once again, as in the early days of church history, a minority movement in a universally antagonistic environment."[3]

In 1947 Fuller Theological Seminary was founded by evangelicals who felt it was time to deal with the liberal voices of the denominational scholars of that time. Carl F. H. Henry further asked, "Is evangelicalism's only message today the proclamation of individual rescue? . . . Or has this evangel implications also for the most pressing social problems of our day?"[4]

The doctrines upon which Fuller was founded were very much the same as the fundamentals of the faith that defined fundamentalism:

> So the fundamental doctrines for which they fought included the
> virgin birth of Christ, his miracles, his bodily resurrection, his sub-
> stitutionary atonement for sin, his second coming. Of particular

importance was the nature of the authority of Scripture. Modernists . . . emphasized the Bible's human origins; fundamentalists countered by affirming its inerrancy in history and science as well as in faith and doctrine.[5]

Inasmuch as there is a written list of the tenets of evangelical faith, this is at least where it all began. In the formation of the term *evangelical*, there were huge arguments whether it should include *antimodernism, dispensationalism,* and *separatism* from other denominations that did not profess these things. Some thought so and some thought not. So this is the basic belief list of evangelicals. However, in a later chapter I mention that when modern evangelicals were polled, only a fraction agreed that they believed in all of these doctrines.

So I agree almost entirely with the shorter definition quoted from "Got Questions" above. Using this looser definition, I have tried to widen the concurrence to speak of evangelicals as those who self-identify as such. Generally speaking, the definition used in this book includes those who have personal faith in Jesus Christ and believe in his atoning sacrifices, miracles, virgin birth, resurrection, and second coming, as well as the all-important doctrine of redemption. Even on these more unitive definitions, there are differences in beliefs on how salvation occurs, the manner of his resurrection, and certainly on the nature of his second coming.

But given our togetherness on these more general and specific issues, you are evangelical the moment you agree to the label. I do agree, and I like the label.

Who Are My Sources?

While this book has relied on a vast amount of sources to support the content, I want to specifically acknowledge a few people who have done more than most to inform my understanding.

First of all, Jacques Barzun, whose magnificent work on culture, *From Dawn to Decadence*, was published in the year 2000 when he was ninety-three years of age. The subtitle of his book is *500 Years of Western Cultural Life from 1500 to the Present*. One reason Barzun can be trusted for a Christian understanding in the West is that he begins his evaluation of our current cultures with the Reformation.

> Look at the youth walking the streets with ears plugged to a portable radio: he is tied to the lives of Marconi and of the composer being broadcast.
>
> Such a youth is a bundle of three tragedies: First, he doesn't care about either Marconi or the composer. Second, he's never heard of them, and third, he could possibly be enrolling in seminary, spreading his ignorance and apathy far and wide, proving that Evangelicalism dies even faster when it is apathetic and uninformed. It is almost impossible to fit Jesus into a world we neither know nor care about.
>
> Jacques Barzun[6]

Barzun's exploration of culture is the premise on which I have proceeded to write. He writes that *decadence is adapting to culture; revolution is forcing the culture to adapt*. More simply put, revolution is an issue of power; decadence is an evidence of powerlessness. Decline always occurs when movements decide to adapt rather than force adaptation on the culture around them. American evangelicalism in every sense is adapting. We look around at secular culture and ask ourselves, "How can we get people to come to church?" The answer is, "Don't ask anything much of them, and rewrite the Christian way of life to look as much like the secular way of life as possible so they can move from one to the other without even flinching." Barzun says, "It takes only a look at the numbers to see that the twentieth century is coming to an end. A wider and deeper scrutiny is needed to see that in the West the culture of the last 500 years is ending at the same time."[7] Naturally, if American evangelicalism is decadent, it becomes further obvious that it is exerting increasingly less change within the culture to which it is accommodating itself. The new form it is taking is too borrowed to be either unique or transformational.

The second primary influence on my reasons for writing this book is Philip Jenkins. His book *The Next Christendom* challenges evangelicals to take a long look at the success we supposed ourselves to be having. Like Barzun, his reflections run back and forth over the past five hundred years. His assessment is:

> We are currently living through one of the transforming moments in the history of religions worldwide. Over the past five centuries or so, the story of Christianity has been inextricably bound up with that of Europe and European-derived civilizations overseas, above all in North America. Until recently, the overwhelming majority of Christians have lived in White nations, allowing theorists to speak smugly, arrogantly, of "European Christian" civilization. Conversely, radical writers have seen Christianity as an ideological arm of Western imperialism. . . . Over the past century, however, the center of gravity in the Christian world has shifted inexorably southward, to Africa, Asia, and Latin America. Already today, the largest Christian communities on the planet are to be found in Africa and Latin America.[8]

In most ways Barzun comments on the Christian culture more as one of the factors of Western (and therefore evangelical) decline. Jenkins, on the other hand, writes directly to the issue of missiology and its ebbing influence in the West. But Western evangelicals in many ways seem to be deluded by their own cultural prominence. They are so dominant in America that they have convinced themselves they have all the vitality.

Secular values, both ethical and medical (not that they are entirely separate), have come to replace Christian

I consider this to be Philip Jenkins's most dismal prophecy:

The stereotype holds that Christians are un-black, un-poor and un-young. If this is true, then the growing secularization can only mean that Christianity is in its dying days. Globally the faith of the future must be Islam.[9]

values in every corner of culture. Sexual cohabitation has overwhelmed our former understanding of committed monogamy. Political correctness and libertinism has replaced every understanding of propriety and cultural modesty. The reasons we put forth to prove we are still a force have to do somewhat with the *emergent church* and even more so the *megachurch*. But size alone cannot give a dying movement vitality. That can only occur through life inherent in real growth by conversions and a thriving missionary conscience. In these areas, as Philip Jenkins denotes, we are woefully lacking.

The final major influence on my thinking has been Thomas Friedman and his weighty volume *The World Is Flat*. I didn't arrive at the importance of his book in one step. I have followed Neil Postman for years, and his book *Technopoly* was for me a stepping-stone into Friedman. But both of them pushed me to the understanding that while technology is the new god of our age, it has brought about a certain *flatness* to all of culture that it touches. Unfortunately, as Friedman confesses, it has not led us to be really creative; instead we are only copycat inventors.

> On December 16, 2005, *The New York Times* carried a story reporting that the average American college graduate's literacy in English had declined significantly over the past decade. . . . Only 31% of graduates demonstrated those high level skills. . . . The literacy of college graduates had dropped because a rising number of young Americans had spent their time watching television and surfing the Internet.
>
> Thomas Friedman[10]

Michael Arguello, a systems architect living in San Antonio, confessed to Friedman, "I taught at a local university. It was disheartening to see the poor work ethic of many of my students. Of the students I've taught over six semesters, I'd only consider hiring two of them. The rest lacked the creativity, problem solving abilities and passion for learning."[11]

One would think the computer revolution would have given evangelicals a new creative force that would have allowed them to conquer the world in better time. Alas, it allowed them only to copy each other's methodologies in worship and even in scholarship. Evangelicals who still had enough faith to want to win people to Christ sublimated their zeal into *computertronics* that led them all to want to write, whether they had anything to say or not, and to imbed their souls in churchy videos that they discarded after only a week or two, moving on to copying someone else's brainchild. Meanwhile, in less techie cultures, a real zeal the American Christians could not imitate was born. Hence in an odd way, serving Friedman's technological philosophy, young evangelicals seem to have taken two wives: the first concubine was Barzun's secular decadence and the second was Friedman's flat earth. Too bad our decline seems to be rooted in such low soil.

After writing her brilliant book *Total Truth: Liberating Christianity from Its Cultural Captivity*, Nancy Pearcey published *Saving Leonardo*, which she subtitled *A Call to Resist the Secular Assault on Mind, Morals and Meaning*. This latter book was insightful as to why contemporary Christianity is succumbing to the secularizing and dehumanizing culture in which Christianity is struggling to hold on to the uniqueness of its voice. I have quoted far less from Robert Bork's *Slouching towards Gomorrah*, probably because it is a slightly older source but nonetheless a hugely insightful work on the moral decay in the West. The same may be said for Neil Postman's *Technopoly*. There are many more books and authors who have influenced me: Christopher Lasch, Dave Tomlinson, Leonard Sweet, and both the Barna Group and the Schaeffer Institute.

For these and the innumerable other pundits I have leaned on, I am most grateful. A purely original book written with no help from the wider world would be mainly worthless. I have also opined and quoted from my own observations as a long-term pastor and professor. My views often come from the frustration of seeing evangelicalism's weak reply to the secular cannonade leveled at it by the current culture.

I am an evangelical. I love all that we are: our heritage, our institutions, our scholars. I adore our free worship, our vehement creativity, our freedom from restrictive traditions, our passion for missions, our courage in the face of debilitating doctrinal attacks. I love our left wing, our right wing, our constantly shifting center. I love the passion we own when we try to speak for God. I love the way we speak for God, when we are sure of ourselves and when we are not. I love the fact that secular politicians have to pay attention to us because it is dangerous to ignore us. I pledge allegiance to our future. I want to stay on this planet as long as I can, just to get a glimpse of what that future will look like. And if the vision is good, I want to help with it. But if we don't do everything right, then this book is written in the hope that we can sometimes do things well. At least we may all endeavor to do them better.

Calvin Miller
Birmingham, Alabama
2012

PART 1

The Current State
of an Inexplicit Gospel

After attending a Christmas Eve service, Larry Crabb wrote:

> The sermon, carefully scripted, but engagingly delivered, also declared a clear message: we can see the face of God in all God's children, in all people, Christian, Jew, Muslim, skeptic, whoever. Conversion isn't necessary. Acceptance is the route to peace. At least that's how I heard it.
>
> The pastor went on. We live in the darkness of exclusivism that brings loneliness and judgment. But the light of Jesus has dawned. And we live in His light when we love all people as they are and open ourselves to being loved in return. I heard nothing to suggest that conversion from something wrong to something right, from lies to truth, from Satan to Jesus, was necessary. If it was, it has already happened, to everyone. The money is already in the bank. All that's left to do is spend it. Don't hate; love. Don't exclude or judge; include, accept. That was the message. . . .

I felt a momentary urge to rip the clip-on microphone off the pastor's robes and shout to the crowd, "Are you saved? Do you realize that the child born in Bethlehem was the man who went to Calvary to die for your sins and mine? Do you really believe that you're nice people enjoyed by a nice God as you live nice lives?"

I suppressed the urge. . . .

Church as I know it usually leaves deep parts of me dormant, unawakened, and untouched.[1]

1. THE EDGE OF RELEVANCE

Every year, 2.7 million church members fall into inactive status. This translates into the realization that people are leaving the church. From our research, we have found that they are leaving as hurting and wounded victims of some kind of abuse, disillusionment, or just plain neglect.

From 1990 to 2000, the combined membership of all Protestant denominations in the United States declined by almost 5 million members (9.5 percent), while the US population increased by 24 million (11 percent).

At the turn of the last century (1900), there was a ratio of 27 churches per 10,000 people, as compared to the close of this century (2000) where we have 11 churches per 10,000 people in America. What has happened?

Given the declining numbers and closures of churches as compared to new church starts, there should have been over 38,000 new churches commissioned to keep up with the population growth.

Richard Krejcir[2]

2. WHEN BIG ISN'T GREAT

At its most basic descriptive level, a megachurch is a congregation that has two thousand or more worship attenders in a week. However, size alone is an insufficient characterization of this distinctive religious reality. The megachurch is a new structural and spiritual organization unlike any other. In order to understand fully the dynamics of megachurches, they must be seen as a collective social phenomenon rather than as individual anomalous moments of spectacular growth or uniquely successful spiritual entrepreneurial ventures.

Scott Thumma[3]

1

The Edge of Relevance

In short, the New Testament writers were completely
consumed with Christ. He was their message, their
teaching, their proclamation, their very life. And everything else flowed out of intimate fellowship with him.

Leonard Sweet and Frank Viola[1]

Futurists sometimes make a decent living by being dour. Optimists
are not as well paid, but they own a rosy talent to see every half-
empty glass as half full. In this book I have tried to live halfway between these extremes. Why? Because I believe the midpoint between
futurism and optimism is realism. Realism is unsettling because it
is that uneasy place where we choose to live and sometimes agree
to feel bad because we don't feel altogether good. I volunteered to
live in this mental state as I wrote this book.

There is a general agreement about the downward spiral of
evangelical vitality and church growth statistics. I suppose there
has been a strong sense of lament amongst all of us who have held

high hopes for all the vitality that once encompassed the movement. One thing seems certain though: there seems no corporate way to save the whole movement. Like most evangelicals, I have hoped and prayed for a grand movement that would stop the bleeding. But I have found not much reward for the hoping. I am reminded of an old bumper sticker I once read: "I'm having a better time since I've given up all hope."

This gloomy forecast I suspect is widespread. George Barna, on whom we all rely a great deal, confessed at the front of the book *Futurecast* that even he has come to believe there will be no grand respite. Since there are no grand highways to resurrection, I feel we must return to the most vital of all possibilities—reformation that begins with the birth of a new individualism that in time may pave a broad way back to our corporate vitality. This is the way people become Christians in the first place: one at a time. Perhaps this one-at-a-time process is the most logical way to return to all we have lost. More about this in the closing chapters.

For now, let me take a strong stand in favor of American evangelicalism. I am an evangelical and love being one, so I have written this book with some reluctance. After all, who wants to criticize his family? I am often asked, "Are you a prophet?" Like Amos of Tekoa, my only answer to the question is, "I [am] neither a prophet nor the son of a prophet" (Amos 7:14). But I have always been good at trend extension, and I am very good at realism. As far as I can see down that road where all evangelicals must soon travel, I am honest. I don't see myself as a change agent of the future, only a reporter of our current milieu. Even so, having examined the trends, my first question is: Where is this slow-down movement called evangelicalism really going? The trend lines do not look good. It's not just the slow-down that bothers me but the rate of the slow-down that is so troubling. Generally I have noticed that the events of any movement that has been moving in one direction continue to move in that direction until they reach a conclusion.

Great movements like American evangelicalism rarely come to a complete and final stop. They end in a reduced state of trickled-down vitality. There will always be evangelicals, of course; the question is how many and for how long?

How Do We Define Evangelicals?

The word *evangelical* is hard to define. Thirty-eight percent of those who refer to themselves as *born again* do not want to refer to themselves as evangelicals. Also, of those adults who say they are evangelicals, 40 percent do not base their salvation on Jesus Christ and his forgiveness. The categories are as hard to pin down as it would be to number Democrats in a US census. These evangelicals or would-be evangelicals move like ghosts in and out of these elusive categories.

What do evangelicals really believe? This is another elusive category.

Robert Bellah, in *Habits of the Heart*, spoke of Sheila, who said she believed in *Sheilaism*.[2] Sheilaism has become the standard doctrine of these days. Among evangelicals, Bill believes in *Billism* and Cindy believes in *Cindyism*.

The Jacques Derrida school of thought is now the rubber-stamp definition of political correctness. The Derrida philosophy states that no truth is true for everyone. Each truth must first be deconstructed and then reconstructed within the worldview of each individual believer. The Nicene Creed (and for that matter the Apostles' Creed) has been replaced by Sheila's creed. We have so altered theology and doctrine

> One thing must be said of *Sheilaism*: it is a doctrine born in suburban sociology and not among the scholars. In the past century as cities sprawled, theology bubbled out across the widening spaces and the new latitudes traded personal permissiveness for theological depth. All constants disappeared.
>
> Robert Bellah[3]

that our creeds must have room to be individualized. The content of those creeds is not based on a religious category—certainly not Sheilaism. On the other hand, when you individualize every creed, is there any real creed left, since creeds themselves are meant to collect individuals into groups of common doctrines? The United Church of God has simplified the Bible and all denominational quarrels by saying that all creeds and confessions boil down to two things, and those two things are a clear focus on God and humankind.

> Everything God requires of his people, and every tenet of right living in the Bible, is founded on two basic principles—loving God and loving our fellow man.
> United Church of God[4]

But what do things look like for the state of the church these days? Pastor Rick Warren has taught us to focus on church health, but what is the real outlook for evangelical health? In a *USA Today* article entitled "More Americans Tailoring Religion to Fit Their Needs," Cathy Lynn Grossman says:

> If World War II–era warbler Kate Smith sang today, her anthem could be "*Gods Bless America*." That's one of the key findings in newly released research that reveals America's drift from clearly defined religious denominations to faiths cut to fit personal preferences and [that] are invalid in any corporate sense. . . . George Barna says, with a wry bit of exaggeration, America is headed for "310 million people with 310 million religions." . . . Barna laments, "People say, 'I believe in God. I believe the Bible is a good book. And then I believe whatever I want.'"[5]

Here's the rub. If it is true that only through individuals can we begin a reformation, can we among our highly individualized sea of believers ever hope for enough unity to pull together any corporate statement of faith that can harmonize the differences? It's a fair question. But without having some tolerance among the eclectic Christian groups, can we ever arrive at the kind of unity it takes to promote missions or ministries of any size or force?

This much we do know: the constants are gone. The Apostles' Creed has changed to: "I believe in God the Father Almighty who, along with the big bang, created the heavens and the earth, and in Jesus Christ his Son, born in the normal x-y chromosomes way." This way, Bible reading always confirms our prejudice and leaves us with that warm fuzzy feeling that God agrees with us on every major point of our privatized doctrine.

The statement about believing the Bible in the quotation above is grossly overestimated. Nearly every evangelical I know, beginning with myself, is quick to say, "I believe the Bible," and most of us read it quite often, yet we never seem to come out at the same place. I have a few pro-choice friends who actually read the Bible and believe it confirms their biases on abortion. The problem is that the Bible is no longer the agreed-upon centerpiece of evangelical thought. Nobody anywhere reads the Bible and comes to anyone else's common agreement. That's because we all read it through a series of filters. Pentecostals read it through Pentecostal filters, reading and seeing mostly what they agree with. So do Baptists and Presbyterians. Baptists who don't believe in women in ministry leadership read quite fast over passages that don't seem to support their views. Episcopalians read the miracle passages more rapidly than do political conservatives in my own denomination.

> While we conservatives were decrying the modern liberal bias, we didn't realize we had developed our own modern conservative bias. We put the Bible through a different colander. The result? Hardly any conservative churches actually encounter the Bible any more. Instead we read edited versions, annotated with commentary, sliced and diced and strained through a number of conservative filters—Dispensational, charismatic, Reformed, whatever.
>
> Brian McLaren and Tony Campolo[6]

Lifeway Research took a survey of nine hundred pastors, 62 percent of whom said that over the next ten years the importance of denominations would diminish greatly. Even now most people have no significant need to be labeled with a denominational tag. Dave Tomlinson and his wife testified that at the Greenbelt Arts Festival in the U.K. they met many attendees who treated the festival as their private church, even though the Greenbelt gathering is only a once-a-year festival.[7]

Corrupting the Evangelical Mission

We have some precedents to guide us through the coming loss of our vitality. As we live through the wake of our decline, in all likelihood we will move in exactly the same downward spiral as other *Christian* nations who have preceded us in their own history of decay.

> These people are just the tip of the iceberg. Tens of thousands of people continue to practice their faith privately while finding no real relevance for the church in their lives.
>
> Dave Tomlinson[8]

Evangelical is a powerful category in American politics. At the ballot box it is a word to be reckoned with—like the words *Tea Party*. But let us take care. Almost all of the nations of Europe still have a Christian Democratic party, but the word *Christian* is an adjective that is more a political modifier than a faith adjective. Could this same destiny await the American adjective *evangelical*? These *God words* remain in our political vocabulary long after they have lost their spiritual force.

The pattern is fixed by precedents. If we accept the trends that have affected others, we will in time also become snared in the whirlpool of our own insipid, privatized faith. Like those we emulate, we will become sluggish, gelid, and comatose. The drift is swift. It was never the intention of British, Canadian, and Australian churches to move so rapidly toward their current lethargic state. After all, it was Britain who in the eighteenth and nineteenth centuries burned with zeal toward missions. They could not in that era of vitality visualize themselves as ever being secularized at such a rapid rate. Canada, in its more rural past, was ablaze with a passion for missions, church growth, and Christian education. Similarly Australia, at the beginning of the twentieth century, was a strong example of missionary passion.

Oddly, our decline may lie in some failures of our missions movement, which sometimes seemed to be as much about exporting Western ideas as it was about taking the gospel to all nations. The problem with the venture was that it was fraught with a traditional mold that rarely stopped to ask whether our traditions and liturgies would really work for the cultures in which we wanted to plant our missionary outposts. As a result, in many of the nations we went to missionize, we only Westernized. And we did that so thoroughly that they often ended up more Western than Christian.

> In author Barbara Kingsolver's hugely successful novel *The Poisonwood Bible*, a missionary girl in the Belgian Congo recollects, "We came from Bethlehem, Georgia, bearing Betty Crocker cake mixes into the jungle."[9]

I can remember seeing an article in a particular missions journal that may explain why Americans met with so much resistance in many non-Christian lands. It told of a Young Girls Auxiliary coronation with African children dressed in formal clothes I'm sure they had taken out of a missions barrel. I remember how odd they looked in the American styles of the times, which never were in vogue in Africa. This never seemed to register with those American missionaries who dressed the African girls in such Western garb.

Beyond Pendulums

Throughout this book I will reiterate this principle: I don't believe in pendulums. I think pendulums themselves are to blame for how I feel about them. I am a mechanical clock lover, and I have three or four of them all ticking away in my home. But these swinging appendages that tick and tock their way through time don't really go anywhere. They just move back and forth, and in truth they are like the movements they emulate: a bit boring. They don't move time, they only measure it. Pendulums were proved by Galileo to be influenced by the geocosmic forces of the planet. I long ago set them aside to opt for a more biblical view of time.

The Bible specifically, and the book of Hebrews generally, reject all views that fashion time as a helix that spirals its way through the centuries, seeming to repeat itself at every turn. On the contrary, the Jews saw time as linear, beginning with God's genesis in creation and moving in a straight line through the law, the prophets, and the gospel to the apocalypse, and then straight ahead to the end of all things. All things? Even American evangelicalism? Yes, even that. No repeats, no returns, no pendulums.

> Galileo is said to have discovered the theory of pendulums during a boring sermon in the cathedral at Pisa when he was seventeen years old. They seem to swing back to where they were, but not quite to where they were. With each swing their arc is diminished, until they do not swing at all. So perhaps Galileo and I are saying the same thing: there is no real return to our previous state of strength.

In the wake of current trends, where every church growth guru encourages us to be discouraged, evangelists who are trying to be upbeat often say, "Don't you think the pendulum will soon swing back?" And I answer their cliché with one of my own: "I don't believe in pendulums!" This usually stops all conversations except from the hyperspiritual, who often quote Matthew 16:18 and say that Jesus promises he is going to build his church on a rock and the gates of hell will not prevail against it. He did say that, and it is true. But this book is not out to refute Jesus. I do, of course, agree with Jesus! There will always be a church, and that church will always grow and show vitality—somewhere.

This book is about American evangelicalism. Jesus didn't found that. It was a subsidiary movement, founded and made in America. The church founded outside of Jerusalem a couple of millennia ago is still in good shape.

In his outstanding book *The Next Christendom*, Philip Jenkins helps us explain ourselves to ourselves. We can read and take some comfort in the fact that while the evangelical church is fading in North America, the church of Jesus Christ is thriving in great numbers in the *global South*.[10] It is there to the south of us where the Lord seems to be adding to the church daily people who are being saved (Acts 2:47). It seems he is no longer adding many new believers on the topside of the globe— up in North America. It makes us sad to have to accede that the good stuff is happening somewhere else in the world. We feel bad that we are the anemic *global North*. We are weary of trying to pump up a sliding cause. Why? Because the lost up where we live can no longer find Christ in the spongy fields of our privatized beliefs.

> Because the Republican Party understands the role of faith in changing society . . . it not only appeals to evangelicals, but it's openly solicitous of their ideas and their opinions. The Democratic Party just does not do that. I do not get any phone calls from Democratic Party leaders, nor their candidates, to inquire as to what evangelicals think. . . . Evangelicals aren't— myths notwithstanding—the GOP of prayer. I mean, we're not. But the Democrats don't even reach out.
>
> Richard Cizik, 2003[11]

The situation is so dire that missiologists now place the United States as the third largest unreached people group (after China and India). What is so unusual about this is that it doesn't look that way. Most of the evangelical cable channels are still intact, just as they were in the 1980s. The Christian book market, while not in full force, is still here. Most major newspapers (which are about the only things doing culturally worse than evangelicalism) still have large religion pages. And ever and anon (every four years at least) most evangelicals vote as a bloc, vastly influencing elections.

Presidential candidates pray! Most of them are openly Christian, and a few of them even have a nice word to say about Jesus.

But there is a certain mustiness about our contrived optimism. And deep down we feel it. Most seminaries wish they were graduating more pastors. Most pastors wish they were seeing more converts. Most denominationalists are troubled by the explosion of house churches. And everyone seems to be stalking that elusive vitality that is so elusive it can terrify us. In our hunger for awakening, we keep hearing Jesus ask, "When the Son of man comes will he find faith on the earth?"

2

When Big Isn't Great

Although the "mega-churches" and "super-churches" bask in the media spotlight, the reality is that most churches in America have fewer than 100 people in attendance on any single day of worship.

George Barna[1]

Big is big news in our time. Big churches, big movements, and a lot of big talk are the companions of our churchy way of life. *Big*, however, is an idea that doesn't mesh well with the decline of evangelicalism. The more we use the word, the smaller we seem to get. There are two big factors that seem to be making us *little*. First, the megachurch—the big church movement—and second, the big ideas that have taken root in our midst. There are three of these big ideologies that affect us: (1) the power of new reformation theology, (2) the tendency of the right to move left, (3) and the new atheism. These big ideas have joined the big church movement to hasten our decline.

The Megachurch and Evangelical Decline

The biggest life sign for evangelicalism is, of course, the megachurch. There are a lot of them, though not compared to other churches (only 1,500 of the nearly 400,000 churches). But they are flashy competitors. When you shoehorn 60,000 evangelicals into the Rose Bowl for an Easter celebration, the media is impressed enough to report the event, which makes all evangelicals proud. But following Easter, we have the odd feeling that we haven't told the whole truth. The whole truth is that we haven't licked the other fifty-one weeks of the year when megachurch attendance, along with that of our not-so-megachurches, is seriously down.

Can we call the growing number of megachurches a real hope for a dynamic revival for all evangelicals? I think not. For one thing there is no unified front among those churches. There is a huge divide, for instance, between the megachurch of John MacArthur and that founded by Rob Bell as well as between those of Rick Warren and Joel Osteen. Not only is their emphasis on doctrine quite different but their worship mystiques are not comparable at all. Most megachurches have so little in common with each other that it seems unlikely there could ever be a sense of corporate vitality among them or their pastors.

> Megachurch pastors are a visible and exotic breed of leaders. While they represent 0.3 percent of North America's churches, they attract about 10 percent of America's weekly evangelical attendees. Most of these churches are high-visibility congregations with national influence and reputation.

The truth is that we have not yet drawn the bottom line on the megachurch. Their histories are all so recent it is not possible to measure their outcome. It was supposedly General Booth who, seeing what complexity and growth had done to the Salvation Army during his lifetime, lamented to his daughter Evangeline, "Why is it that God cannot seem to keep an organization pure above a generation or so?" It is that kind of evaluation that takes some history to observe, and it is precisely that kind of record the megachurch has yet to measure. We evangelicals have had our fads and have often depended on the interest these nuances create to bolster our life signs.

But in previous decades we have moved from glossolalia, to exorcisms, to pyramidal schemes like some sort of *Jesus-Amway* movement. Although the megachurch is too substantial to be labeled a fad, we are still too much at the front of it to really measure whether it will long endure.

What are its weaknesses? First, it is so rooted in the rock-concert deportment of our age that it looks a bit shaky. The danger with tying yourself too closely to contemporary culture is that all culture is transient and too unstable to form a foundation for any movement that is to endure.

Second, its strongest attraction is that it affords mostly anonymity, not community. In a culture where every novel and sitcom is about the search for community, the megachurches provide too little. These churches often brag that they promote anonymity. "People want to go to church and be left alone." It sounded so good. But in the end, turning away from "Will every visitor please stand up," and "Come to the altar and get right with God," asks so little of the seekers they quit seeking! Perhaps this is why megachurches experience such a large turnover of visitors with so many first-time attendees merely looking around before they move on.

Finally, they are underfunded, with too few giving too little to provide enough real supporters of the church. The megachurch doesn't understand this short truth: what doesn't cost people in the end doesn't hold people.

Some years ago one of our finest church members, who was a single businessman, moved to Chicago. He soon became involved in the church of *what's happening now*. Before long he met a young woman and became engaged. After they had set the date for their marriage, he called me—his former pastor—and asked if I would come to Chicago to tie the knot. "Of course," I said. "But what about your senior pastor?"

"Well," he said, "I don't really know him."

"Well then, what about your assistant pastor?"

"Well, I don't know him either."

"Okay," I said. "Will you be married in the church's chapel?"

"Well . . . no," he said. "It's booked for the next year. We've rented a little Lutheran church down the street. Is that okay?"

"Sure," I said. "So are you telling me that you love your church, but it is not of real help when you really need it?"

"I guess so."

I flew to Chicago and married them in a Lutheran church. They were married there but have long since joined another church.

So why am I bringing up the megachurch as a factor in evangelical decline? Surely it should not be written off as a fad. Although evangelicals may deny being influenced by the large-church trend and postdenominational detente, these basic cultural laws really seem to be the force behind most of the church growth vision statements I have read. Megachurches offer a contribution of contemporary music and highly relevant sermons, which often means sermons that outline successful living and even corporate success in the eclectic world of the current, fast-paced culture. For the most part, these sermons do not focus on transcendent themes. Evangelists still call their preaching *expository*, but often, contemporary sermons focus on

Contemporary worship music is a loosely defined genre of Christian music used in contemporary worship. It has developed over the past sixty years and is stylistically similar to pop music. The songs are frequently referred to as "praise songs" or "worship songs" and are typically led by a "worship band" or "praise team," with either a guitarist or pianist leading. It is a common genre of music sung in Western churches, particularly in Pentecostal churches, both denominational and nondenominational.

"Contemporary worship music," Wikipedia[2]

sparsely studied biblical texts while the amplifiers talk big and the Bible has laryngitis.

The Importance of *Big*

While most megachurches may cite their purist views of Scripture and the kingdom of God as the reason for their growth, I am not the first to ask if they are actually more influenced by American corporate theory. We evangelicals sometimes seem to be only the religious arm of the secular, corporate mentality. Big buildings are the way we say to IBM or Ford Motors, "We Christians are big too! Look at our buildings. Come in and succeed in your religious life just as you have in your corporate life. Be big with us. Be Christian in a major way. Succeed on Sunday too." Our political group dynamics scream from interstate billboards that we are on the rails of success just as Jesus intended.

Decades ago Mircea Eliade said that the sacred and the secular have vastly different sights and sounds.[3] The more the two become indistinguishable, the weaker the sacred becomes, until ultimately it dies out in favor of the secular. What he is trying to say is that when you turn on a radio station, you have to really listen to determine whether you are hearing a Christian Three Dog Night or an evangelical Lady Gaga. Lady Gaga is winning. This means that if you are in a concert hall and it is filled with smoke and strobes and you have to keep asking yourself, "Is this all for Jesus?" it probably isn't really.

And the bigger question that must be asked is: Since evangelicalism is so secular in its deportment, will it survive, and if so, what form will it take in the future? Is the fact that evangelicalism is so customary these days an evidence of cultural strength, or is it more an evidence that we are attending the wedding of the Apostles' Creed and Woodstock? And the more this secular-religious marriage is celebrated, could it be that the megachurch so much resembles the culture that it is powerless to change it?

Big is the all-American adjective. Woodstock and the megachurch both wear it. If New Testament history is any comment, however, the large crowds attracted by the preaching of Peter or the theologically ill-informed Apollos did not have the effect of Paul, who preached to very small crowds when he wasn't in jail. And it has been well said that while Jesus founded the church, Paul defined it. Blot Apollos's name out of Christian history and you have only a big meeting that appears in every age to be more of a rally than worship. But blot Paul's name out of history and half of the New Testament does not exist.

But remember this: huge churches are not the sole property of American evangelicalism. In one of the more dowdy areas of London, far from Piccadilly, lies the near-ruins of the old Spurgeon tabernacle. It has burned down a couple of times and been rebuilt, much smaller each time, until it no longer resembles the nineteenth-century megachurch it used to be. Subtract the fire, and the same could be said of the Billy Sunday tabernacle in Winona Lake, Indiana. These once huge establishments are not entirely dead. They all have bookstores and curio shops (they are always the last things to die), and a comparatively few stragglers still attend there. Spurgeon's old tabernacle has become a haven for Calvinistic Baptists. But Baptists have been unable to make Calvinism take off; they still try to sell it in the rock-and-roll culture they have so reluctantly inherited.

There is one place where the megachurch has ill-defined the importance of *Big*. The key issue of this question is community. To be upfront, the core issue that could most hasten our decline is that fewer and fewer people find the church a place of community. From the twentieth-century church, when families found a way of life, to the twenty-first-century church when the hunger for anonymity brought the desertion of the family, people have learned that there is no place to plug in to the church to meet all their needs for community.

Three Emphases That Contribute to Evangelical Decline

Every generation contains within it ideological emphases that will define and determine the ebb and flow of the faith and practice of our families, churches, and ministries within the Christian community. We have looked at the megachurch and its leaders, but there are other tangents of evangelical thought that have enough popularity

> Paul's view of what is called Reformed theology:
>
> "Those he predestined, he also called; those he called, he also justified; those he justified, he also glorified."
> Romans 8:30
>
> Paul's view of a less-structured, more random mystery of God:
>
> "Oh, the depth of the riches of the wisdom and knowledge of God! How unsearchable his judgments, and his paths beyond tracing out!"
> Romans 11:33

in their own right to do significant damage to what should be the focus of evangelicalism and its leadership. I wish to examine three which are eroding the "simplicity and purity of devotion to Christ" and they are complicating or diluting evangelicalism until we no longer know who we are or what we should be.

1. Rise of Reformed Scholarship

Every religious group has had its deterministic wing, which allows people to excuse themselves from responsibility for their faults because they are their destiny. This provides answers to all questions but kills the mystery in which they come wrapped. Also, let's not forget that the New Testament was born in the midst of Greco-Roman religion, which claimed there were no mysteries because every puzzlement was solved in some myth. Then they were replaced by the glorious mysteries—at first called *mystery religions*—that came with ultimate meaning but not many answers.

Jesus is founder and the God-man keeper of all our particular Christian saving mysteries. How can a man be born without genetics or walk out of the tomb alive after three long days? We are redeemed by things too excellent for our understanding.

Many of the new reformation pastors I know do not like to be called the new reformation, and they despise the prefix *neo*, as in *neo-Calvinism*. Most of them still harken back five centuries to John Calvin, saying there is nothing *neo* about them; they are tied firmly to John Calvin himself. But they have willingly adopted a scholarly narrowness that at times keeps their heads buried in the scholarship of the past, and they are not necessarily informed of the arts or the mysteries or our own times.

The fastidiousness with which they pursue their dialectic may have displaced the fervor and passion of evangelistic qualities more than they realize—especially in small Reformed churches in which the art of worship and creative planning is not in place. As a point of reference for Calvinism and the arts, we need to go back to the beginning of the Reformation in the sixteenth century. Some of the Protestant Reformers, in particular Andreas Karlstadt, Huldrych Zwingli, and John Calvin, encouraged the removal of religious images by invoking the prohibition of idolatry and the manufacture of graven images in the Ten Commandments.

It was a true iconoclasm. Calvinism, it seems, has always had more of an interest in creating dialectic than art. This is unfortunate because cultures define themselves through art, not dialectic. A single piece of Phoenician pottery tells us who the Phoenicians were, how they lived, and what they esteemed. Dialectic, on the other hand, only fills books that in time hold less-usable information.

What about hyperscholarship is hastening our decline? Not much you can put your finger on, but it seems that passion and study do vary immensely. Revivals and awakenings feed on fervor and spontaneity, not intense study. So the rise of neo-Calvinism may be impeding results more than its proponents know. It seems true at least that the success of Christianity in the global South wins the case in point. These cultures are growing awash in fervor, but perhaps they are not much marked by Reformed scholarship.

I have had the honor of being a teacher during the last couple of decades when the Reformed resurgence has been swelling. These students found excitement in their studies, and so they should have, but in the process they left the world that founded them in faith. What's so bad about that? Well, in many ways the church they left was generally more schooled in making converts than the graduate school they entered. Seminaries—and I have worked in two of them—are places of discourse about evangelism, but sometimes as a whole they don't create the social matrix in which it takes place.

> There are many Christians who do not feel his glorious presence as something real, because for them Jesus occurs in their minds and not in their hearts. Only when someone surrenders his heart to Jesus can he find him.[4]

Evangelism and church planting courses are present in seminaries, but it is assumed that what the seminary teaches is for the students' use somewhere out there beyond the degree. Out there in the suburbs, often the megachurch methodologies have a chance to hatch. These sluggish methodologies may unwittingly contribute to the decline of evangelicalism.

2. The Trend of the Right to Move Left

This killing evangelistic entropy is a kind of built-in law of life and death. The odd thing is that almost all evangelical seminaries were founded for the major purpose of evangelism and missions. But once established, they gradually became interested in trusts and endowments, academic certifications, and denominational status. Thus they are all too prone to trade fire for reputation. There is something in the heart of the right that ever moves left, but there is nothing in the heart of the left that ever moves right.

Liberty University[5] longs for status and reputation, and while they would decry their march toward liberalism (and it may take a hundred years or so), it is also moving in that direction. But there are none at Harvard Divinity School who want to move back toward the founding principles. They are quite content to be broader than that, and thus every movement ever marches *brainward* from the heart. It is probably also true that the more a religion moves brainward, the more likely it is to lose *vitality*—a kind of synonym for *life*.

Of course the conservatism that hatched evangelicalism is becoming liberated at a good clip. Rob Bell (and others) have of late jettisoned the concept of hell—something his forebears in 1950 would never have considered. John Piper, who sees Bell's universalism as a heresy (as it is), remarked tersely, "Farewell, Rob Bell!" This new liberalism on the right is killing the passion required to keep evangelicals from declining.

Much of the emergent church movement, which grew out of the church growth mentality, is becoming more liberal, and their liberalism is hastening the decline of vitality. This emergent church liberalism emanated from the conservative end of Christianity rather than the liberal end. But no matter where it came from, it seems to be contributing to evangelical decline.

3. The Face of the New Atheism and Its Influence on Decline

I don't want to dwell on this long, but my personal convictions forced me to speak of the *new atheists*, who are having such an influence today. Atheism has been around at least since the fourteenth psalm was written: "The fool has said in his heart, 'There is no God'" (Ps. 14:1 NKJV). But as evangelical influence weakens, it seems to be growing ever more virulent. The late Charles Colson recently wrote:

> Surveying the press coverage over the last couple of years makes it clear that Christianity is reeling from a bruising and unprecedented attack by aggressive atheism. . . . In 2006, Richard Dawkins, a clever

and articulate Oxford evolutionary biologist, published *The God Delusion*, which took up a near permanent residence on the *New York Times* bestseller list. Dawkins considers religious instruction a form of child abuse and suggests that governments should put a stop to it.[6]

A similar book to Dawkins's was written by Christopher Hitchens (*God Is Not Great*), and a great many more atheists are advancing in an ever-growing army. This is no longer a fringe phenomenon. According to the *Wall Street Journal*, these authors sold close to a million books in one twelve-month period alone. Richard Dawkins, who is responsible for half of those sales, can attest to how lucrative attacking God has become.

Atheistic zealots. Ordinarily I would not consider these voices to have any long-term triumph. But driven by the winds of political correctness and the weakening vitality of evangelicalism, I believe they are a new kind of force that must be reckoned with.

Conclusion

Perhaps we evangelicals are the victims of our own lust for church growth. The megachurch along with the three movements of the rise of the new reformation, the secular forces that have moved the church even more to the left, and to a lesser extent the secularizing force of the virulent new atheists have all moved us from the simple pursuit of our evangelistic calling. It is odd that we never stopped talking about church growth, only our calling to evangelize. In the end we never quit desiring church growth, but the loss of our evangelistic zeal was the very thing that stole our will to grow. Dying is the natural result of not really caring about life.

PART 2

Believing Enough to Survive

As a pastor I feel the need to caution my peers who might unwittingly lead people into thinking they have a relationship with God just because they repeated a prayer or raised their hand in an invitation.

Not long ago I listened to someone preach a powerful message about the good news that God saves all who confess their sins and turn to Jesus Christ. When he concluded, he implored all those who did not have a relationship with God to respond by repeating a prayer after him. After leading his listeners in a straightforward prayer, he confidently declared that everyone who had just repeated his prayer was now a child of God.

I winced. But not because I thought God hadn't saved anyone who repeated that prayer. On the contrary, I believed with all my heart that those who had honestly confessed their need for God that day began a relationship with him that will last forever. Rather I winced because the preacher based his promise that God saved them on an external ritual rather than an internal reality.

Tullian Tchividijian[1]

3. A PASSION OF PRETENSE, A WORSHIP OF DISINTEREST

A generation of young Christians believes that the churches in which they were raised are not safe and hospitable places to express doubts. Many feel that they have been offered slick or half-baked answers to their thorny, honest questions, and they are rejecting the "talking heads" and "talking points" they see among the older generations.

David Kinnaman[2]

4. SNUGGLING IN WITH CULTURE

The Christian mind in America was never more remarkable than in its earliest days, when society was not settled and the conditions were hazardous and far from secure. To our shame it is the secular mind, not the Christian mind, that has expanded most fruitfully in the settled conditions of later times. There is a grand irony in the fact that we evangelicals are citizens in a republic whose revolution was led by intellectuals and are disciples in a community of faith whose reformation was led by intellectuals—yet we are the epitome of anti-intellectualism and proud of it.

Os Guinness[3]

3

A Passion of Pretense, a Worship of Disinterest

I ask no dream, no prophet ecstasies,
No sudden rending of the veil of clay,
No angel visitant, no opening skies;
But take the dimness of my soul away.

George Croly[1]

"In the last generation, with public Christianity in headlong retreat, we have caught sight of our first, distant view of a de-Christianized world, and it is not encouraging."[2] So said Paul Johnson in the mid-1970s. But Gallup, having long measured church vitality, invites us to consider how far we have fallen:

Studies conducted by Gallup and others a half century or more ago confirm that church involvement was a given in those days. During the tumult of the 1960s, people began to seriously question the value of all institutions and cultural norms, including the value of church

45

life. Americans continue to question the value of many traditional institutions and lifestyle habits, one of which is how best to further their spiritual objectives.[3]

But the central objective of the church is and has always been worship.

What then is the picture of where our worship is in the fifty years since Gallup's statistics seemed to be on our side (if you're on the evangelical side of hope)? Consider the long haul. In this long, fifty-year gap, it gets easier to see whence we have fallen. Remember, however, that there is no pendulum. Concerning our lost passion for real worship, we are no more likely to swing back to our previous state of health than was England or Sweden.[4] Regardless, the decline in the fervency of our worship is not encouraging. Every eye is on the statistical charts; church growth researchers have added to our depressive outlook on recovering our lost vitality. Why? Because they have kept our eyes focused on the statistics of our dying. We are like patients attended by a thousand medical technicians, each measuring our pulse, our breathing, and our weakening anemia, and writing down the grim facts of our diminishing vitality. If there is any possibility of an attendance revival in the evangelical church, it is rarely brought up. Watching our dying is sometimes ghoulish, but it is also fascinating.

But the constant observation of our condition does not heal it. Gallup's 1960 observations measured an evangelicalism rooted in strong loyalties to individual congregations. George Barna laments that long-lost fidelity: "About one-third of regular churchgoers now visit multiple churches—not so much as an exercise in church hopping, but to see if they can find God moving somewhere in their community."[5] This is our longing after worship.

Why the lost vitality in worship? We should be quite alive. We should be proud of the fact that we are still in the life-and-death business of passion and worship. After all, we are still bringing our dangerous message to a needy world. I believe there is a direct correlation between passion in worship and denominational vitality. *Dying* keeps a pecking order.

The Episcopalians are dying faster than the Assembly of God. Baptists are declining slower than the Methodists. Generally the right-side evangelicals are thriving more than the moderate Presbyterians. And even those we used to call cults don't seem to be taking their raison d'etre very seriously. The Jehovah's Witnesses are staying inside during the dog days of August—and

> Bill Hybels suggested that the church should be a safe place to hear a dangerous message. Annie Dillard said that the church should be a "danger zone" with orange cones and sawhorse barriers saying something like, "Enter at your own risk. A holy God is in this place."

their once-upon-a-time marriage of zeal and door-to-door methodology lately seems less zealous.

Mormons, who have taken a few chops to the chin in the Broadway musical *The Book of Mormon*, do seem to be thriving. Few American Protestant denominations today can refer to themselves as healthy and growing. Even so, if you can't call yourself a growing denomination, you can at least brag that you're dying slower than other Christian groups. Often this has led the various plateaued groups to feel smug around those whose health they outshine and humble around those whose vitality is stronger than their own.

George Barna is the grand statistician of all the dying. In one of his more recent books, *Grow Your Church from the Outside In*, he divides the contemporary church attenders into five groups:[6]

1. The *unattached* are the people who have not attended any church service or program within the last year. This group is 23 percent of the adult population, about a third of which have never attended any church. Is there a correlation between their disinterest and the overall reputation that churches have boring worship?

2. The *intermittents* constitute about one out of every seven adults (15 percent of Americans). They have gone to church at

least once during the past year, but not necessarily the past month. Is it nonvital worship that causes intermittents to be intermittent?

3. The *homebodies*—about 3 percent of adults—are those who have not attended a conventional church during the past month but have attended a house church. Are the growing numbers of house-church worshipers rejecting just the organized church or the worship they fail to make vital?

4. *Blenders* have attended both a conventional church and a house church during the past month, and they also comprise about 3 percent of the population. Blenders seem to be searching for a place to worship that offers them the most comfortable place to snuggle into the survival mode.

5. *Conventionals* make up about 56 percent of the population. They attend and either tolerate or enjoy the worship of the traditional churches at least once or more each month.

This survey reflects a distaste for worship, and it is not at all encouraging. When we first spotted the symptoms of our malaise, we could tell ourselves, "Next year things will get better." But next year was not better. The lingering fear is that the trend is destined to push American religiosity into the same poor church attendance that long ago became typical of Europe and England and that has clearly begun to take root in New England and both the eastern and western seaboards of the United States. Is the decline caused by just a distaste for church or the worship in a church?

> I've always been a pretty regular churchgoer. I used to be a Congregationalist—I was baptized in the Congregational Church, and after some years of fraternity with Episcopalians (I was confirmed in the Episcopal church too), I became rather vague in my religion: in my teens I attended a "nondenominational" church. Then I became an Anglican; and the Anglican Church of Canada has been my church ever since I left the United States, about twenty years ago.
>
> *A Prayer for Owen Meany*
> by John Irving[7]

Recently, in order to encourage a return of their summer vacation absentees, the churches have instituted a back-to-church emphasis in the fall. They admit that people who drop out of worship for the summer meander back into the flock very slowly once vacation time is over. But it isn't just the old-line denominationalists who have lost their passion for worship. Faithfulness and vitality are ebbing among even the more fiery and conservative denominations as well. The alarm clock is now shut off on Saturday nights. The faithful are lackadaisically sleeping through that numbing dullness called the Sunday homily.

> Within my lifetime, I have seen the fulfillment of every sign Jesus gave his disciples 2,000 years ago. Not only have I seen the signs, but I have observed the local, national, and global *birth pains* increase in astonishing frequency and intensity. I am convinced that the kingdoms of this world are about to give birth to the kingdom of God.
>
> Anne Graham Lotz[8]

Anne Graham Lotz, tired of the faddish adjectives that evangelicals apply to themselves from time to time, seems to react in particular to the word *postmodern*. She begs evangelicals to ditch the hyperintellectualism and pseudophilosophical rhetoric and cry, "Just give me Jesus!" I understand her point, and I too think we often use high-sounding arguments to keep our minds off our dying vitality.

But it is not just church attendance we have lost; we have dropped a way of life that our devout worship once held in place. There are two specific areas that have sped the pace of our decay: (1) loss of interest in traditional Christian worship and substantive discipleship, and (2) postmodernism.

The Loss of Interest in Worship and Discipleship

Peter Kreeft's 1980 definition of *worship* still rings true for me: Worship never is the end in itself; it is the freedom to let go of our joy and turn it all back to God. This is not done to glorify ourselves as we speak of God, and we must be careful not to focus too much on ourselves. "Joy in our spirit does not stay there, bottled up and stagnant. Spirit is essentially dynamic, and its joy flows out in three directions: back to God in gratitude and rejoicing, out to others like a watering fountain, and into our own souls as a sort of overspill . . . this is a foretaste of heaven."[9] The more we evangelicals focus on ourselves instead of God, the more our joy is diminished. The more joy is diminished, the easier it is to wander away from fervent faith.

> The home of joy is God. . . . Another divine attribute seems to be that it has no finite opposite. . . . Pleasure has a finite opposite: pain. Happiness has a finite opposite: unhappinesss or sadness. But joy has no imaginable finite opposite, for joy is of itself infinite.
>
> Peter Kreeft[10]

But the critical distinction—the big question—is: Is this really involved in the degeneration of evangelicalism? I believe that it is. People will not seek to make their way to a God who is losing his divine status in the eyes of the worshipers. We are not attracted to a God who is so much on our level that we see no need to seek him out. So how can he help us very much?

I suspect the contemporary church with its emphasis on all things contemporary—including worship—may have become ensnared in a form of cultural narcissism. I remember when I first began to see contemporary singers getting familiar with God. At first I was stunned, but as time passed, I got used to it to the point that they seemed authentic when they dressed like rock stars and crammed the microphone nearly down their throats to create a recognizable secular feel for their musical drama. I can't help but ask, however: Who are we celebrating here? Then from that point, the amps grew louder and the smoke machines belched ever denser clouds of mist. Colored lights and mirror balls quickly followed.

I have never known an avant-garde worship leader who did not think he or she was doing God service by using a new *Vegas-esque* apparatus. As they see it, it is a way of reaching out to the heart of the culture (the eighteen- to twenty-nine-year-olds). Most of them were not fake, just naive. They genuinely felt that Jesus was leading them to make church appealing to a new generation. And since they sang and swayed in popular contemporary churches, it was clear they felt that the electric Jesus was an effective worship communication. To them the evangelicalism they projected seemed anything but declining. It seemed to be exploding. Their keyboards and drums moved right into the midst of those who were trying to reach out to their apocalyptic age.

They genuinely felt there was something redeeming in their calling. They hoped to keep the old hymn-singing fuddy-duddies from ruining the church's ability to reach the switched-on culture. And they knew their own world well enough to reach out more effectively than the older saints did.

There are two flaws in their reasoning. The first flaw is that the new musicians are not as schooled in theology as they are in communication. Their sins are unintentional. And if you apply their worship only to numbers, they come out big winners. But if you look at the long-term bottom line, they may have removed God from his traditional box and repackaged him in strobe lights and fog machines.

Their second flaw is that they do not understand that their forebears didn't write their hymns because they wanted to be contemporary. They wrote and sang them because they were spiritually needy and were seeking to the best of their ability to lift up Christ and thus make the ills of their world more bearable. They weren't trying to save Christianity from its traditions; they were trying to learn what their forebears knew and offer it as healing for their own times.

I have always thought it odd that so many of the megachurch worship leaders smugly feel they have done it right. This is obvious when they *brag up* their worship. At the huge worship conferences where they teach others their art, they speak of how long it takes them to plan their worship and how they set it all up as theatrically

51

> Next Sunday, as you drive through your community, if you observe all the cars in the church parking lots and breathe a sigh of relief, deciding that all is well—you're just fooling yourself. If you are not examining the why, what, and how of your spiritual life, you are in the minority. The cumulative outcome of those ruminations will produce a religious landscape—and even a Christian church—that bears a surprisingly limited resemblance to the church world of 2000.
>
> George Barna, *Futurecast*[11]

as possible to *wow*. Without realizing it, many of them have ceased to worship God and begun to worship their worship. I have often heard an extremely creative worship captain say, "We have the most creative worship in our area"—as though that is the goal. The real danger is that for many I suspect it is the goal. It works as a kind of religious narcissism. Such none-too-vital worship sometimes leads them at first to temporary, numerical success. But things change, and in a very few years things that seemed cutting-edge become irrelevant.

The Postmodern Factor

The second area that has sped the pace of our decay is the influence of postmodernism—not just on religion but on every area of worship. Postmodernism runs the same course as deconstructionism, which—as we said in the introduction—teaches that no single truth is true for all people. This means that every apparent truth needs to be broken down into its simpler parts and reconstructed within the psyche of each person, leaving it up to the individual to determine whether any single truth is acceptable to him or her. Corporate worship constants become fuzzy at best. As we said previously, such a philosophy renders meaningless all attempts to found an orthodoxy everyone can agree on. And it also struggles to find a kind of worship everyone can agree on. Old corporate-worship confessions may still be mouthed in unison, yet the interpretations of the individualized elements of that worship confession would hardly be held in common agreement.

Therefore, the weakening of evangelical orthodoxy lies in the sovereignty of each individual believer, for there is no corporate confession upon which we all agree. We continue to mouth the creeds, but if pinned down, we're not all that sure we agree to all the verities we confess. The truth of the biblical account is considered highly fanciful by some, and the part of orthodoxy that keeps them coming back to the church is much simpler and more intact with everyday logic than with the mystery that hides in the heart of real biblical teaching. The same goes for the morality and ethics of Scripture. Most postmodern Christian worshipers construct their personal faith from truths they want to hold as their own *privatized* confession.

> When Jesus came to the Jordan where John was baptizing and stepped down into the water, fire blazed up in the Jordan.
>
> Justin Martyr[12]

So postmodernism becomes merely a gelatinous framework of *my homemade definition of worship* versus *your homemade definition of worship*. Should the Apostles' Creed be checked at the vestibule door? The worship confession of the church is sometimes no more than an annoying repetition of somebody's ideas about God rather than a collective declaration.

The only problem I see with "Just give me Jesus" is that the entreaty does not always keep in touch with the evangelistic force of a Wesley crying, "Give me England or I die." "Just give me Jesus" begs us search for the Christ we have lost. But where was he lost? At the heart of our worship. And how can we lose the object of our worship in corporate worship? Because we have dressed him too much in secular camouflage until we can no longer find him. Oh that we had him back. He was the Christ of force. He was Justin Martyr's force of fire. We agree that we should win people to Christ, but we have lost the Christ to whom we should win them. Only if it is possible to find and preach that Christ can we hope to slow the decline.

Christian apologetics was once the grand attorney of the church. It was in a sense the authority of our worship. It reasoned and won its day in court. It defended and protected the flock of God—the sheep who didn't read as much had a more informed *apologist-protector*; the unthinking ones had a *thinking protector*. The more virile apologists of the 1960s and '70s championed books like *Evidence That Demands a Verdict*.[13] It was a brilliant catalogue of the consistent confessions of orthodoxy.

> The fuel for evangelicalism is not so much running out as the increasing longing for God is making fuel unnecessary. What used to matter to evangelicalism doesn't matter anymore—not because it isn't true, but because it's obsolete.
> Mike Yaconelli[14]

But by the rise of the postmodern Christian culture of the 1990s, there was no single view of orthodoxy to defend. "The Four Spiritual Laws," Campus Crusade's ten-minute argument for making converts, fell into a kind of weak dispute about its legal tone in a culture that has rejected all *laws*, including spiritual ones. People who read *Evidence That Demands a Verdict* began asking, "Excuse me; was that my verdict or your verdict?"

Postmodernism exalts the individual to be the keeper of his or her own worship. Biblical authority is the loser. There is one vital question for each worshiper that has remained the same down through the ages: Do you believe the Bible? A simple yes would do. But the latter-day worshiper answers, "I believe the Bible as I understand it." The liturgy is still in place, but it doesn't always represent the believer's true hunger for the passion of worship.

A couple of years ago I was speaking to a large Lutheran assembly and very much enjoying their worship. I was particularly intrigued by the liturgy of their corporate confession, which is a highly biblical understanding of confession and gut-level basics. But such stark openness about sin and redemption led me to wonder what each of the confessors really believed about sin and their own confession. They seemed quite comfortable and didn't appear to believe themselves in any real danger of judgment.

The postmodern grasp on our confession means that there is an ever-widening gap between orthodoxy and orthopraxy—what we *believe* is nowhere close to what we are actually *living out*. This, of course, amounts to whether we practice what we preach. Herein lies the abyss. Preaching hasn't changed a great deal since the nineteenth century, but preachers have.

The number one reason for the weakening vitality is that behind our bilious rhetoric there is no prophet. The doctrine of salvation according to postmodern preachers is not, "Repent and believe and you will be saved," but, "Repent generally and believe casually, and you may be saved, depending on how much danger you believe yourself to be in. But above all, keep what you really believe to yourself. Nobody else agrees with you anyway."

The Decline of Value in Arts and Entertainment

We who have inherited the past five hundred years of post-Reformation Christianity can see how, for all our ardent missionary passion, we have walked away from art and artists. It is hard not to look at the grudge most of the Reformers felt for the arts and not realize how their passion for preaching and missions was not accompanied by an equal passion to give Christianity an artistic voice. Concerning the Reformation, Barzun writes:

> With each new sectarian reform, the houses of worship became more and more bare of ornament. Luther did not object to flowers, nor did he, like some of the zealots, want to break the stained glass of ancient churches or vandalize the sculptures. But pictures and altar cloths, candles and relics, and the crucifix must go, incense

too, and the priests' vestments. . . . It was, said the English Puritans and Presbyterians, "Idolatry dressed up."[15]

Oddly, as we lost our influence in the arts, we seem to have lost our power to influence the culture. That loss of power to influence is the force behind the decline.

Maybe that happened because we failed to realize the unbreakable bond that exists between worship and art. Ayn Rand was right when she said that art is "man defining himself." But it is hard to see much of evangelical worship as art. Much of our worship is so bad that most of us don't want it to be our self-definition. Indeed, who among us call it art? It is a question every worship leader should ask himself or herself. Art isn't just a self-definition; it is a struggle for excellence in self-definition.

> It is said that George Bernard Shaw was asked to review a play, which he saw and panned. When asked if there was nothing positive he could say about the play, he quipped, "The scenery was good, but the actors kept getting in front of it."

For instance, some of the worst forms of Christian art I have seen are in cowboy churches. I once heard a Christian yodel her glory to God, and later in the same service, I heard a Roy Rogers impersonator sing "Happy Trails to You." Many, if not most, religious sages feel that religion is most vigorous and healthy when it has the power to influence the morality of a culture, not merely imitate it.

Preachers also should know the struggle for excellence at the heart of our adoration. But preaching as an art form isn't doing all that well either. When religions divide into subcultures and try to become a path to all vitality, they generally advance decline.

In his splendid book *From Dawn to Decadence*, Jacques Barzun describes what has happened to us in one magnificent idea. He defines *decadence* as adapting to culture and *revolution* as forcing culture to adapt. From this simple definition it is easy to see that from Billy Sunday to Billy Graham and on to today, Christianity has been moving from revolution to decadence. And of our own times and culture, Barzun opines, "When people accept futility and the absurd as normal, the culture is decadent. The term is not a slur; it is a technical label."[16]

Decadence has arrived in full force in our time. The complacent theology of our day has lost its virility. Robert Bork is right: we really are "slouching towards Gomorrah." An anemic evangelicalism seems powerless to call biblical faith back to its lost stamina. Unfortunately, evangelicalism has opted to adapt without understanding that to adapt is to die.

> In the nineteenth century, the problem was that God is dead; in the twentieth century, the problem is that man is dead.
> Erich Fromm[17]

Erich Fromm, reflecting on the roots of the God Is Dead movement, said there is one thing worse than God being dead—it is that humans are now dead with a kind of death that is not easily resurrected. In fact, bringing the culture back from spiritual death requires a worship vitality that we probably can no longer muster.

To live, on the other hand, is to struggle with the art of worship until our passion wins the day. Until those who come for worship share our sincerity and our depth of soul. Until they see in our hymns and liturgies that we are a people who are caught up in our love affair with God. Erich Fromm suggests that when we are dead, we give people the impression that God is dead.

Conclusion

In our weekly staff meetings at the church I once pastored, we were forced to see the truth about the rise and fall of our weekly church attendance. As we evaluated what brought a spike or a drop in our attendance, we tried to highlight the weather, a flu outbreak, or a lack of promotion for an event that we really wanted to work. But we usually admitted that we were giving only mechanical answers to spiritual problems. Once we were honest, we admitted we probably were suffering from a lack of ardor or passion. Perhaps this fundamental issue needs to be published far and wide. If you build it, they may or may not come. But if they come and catch you at worship—real worship—they will not only come, they will come back regularly.

Worship is power we hold over the world. Done well, the mystery of godliness draws the hungry to our table.

4

Snuggling in with Culture

Defending the Moral Majority, Tim LaHaye referred to Gallup's 1980 survey that said there were 60,000,000 born-again believers living in America. There were another 60,000,000 who were what he called "promoralists" (Catholics, Mormons, and so on). Then there were another 50,000,000 "idealistic moralists." That represents 84% of the people of this country who still believe the Ten Commandments are valid.[1]

There has been a long-standing argument about just how closely morality and religion are related. Generally, sociological liberals say that religion doesn't necessarily influence behavior and vice versa. I have read much on the issue of morality and its influence on faith, and I remain convinced that faith and moral behavior do influence each other. The exact connection between the Columbine School massacre and the movie *Rambo* is difficult to prove, and the recent wave of flash mobs turning to teen violence cannot be connected to the issues of drug abuse in concrete ways. But most evangelicals believe there is a definite connection between active faith and good behavior.

In the popular teenage, sexual-abstinence program called "Why Wait Till Marriage?" teens who went against the safe-sex doctrine of careful indulgence seemed to demonstrate that their own *faith priorities*, particularly as related to a person's salvation in Christ, were better able to carry out their own commitment to chastity. But are these young people being prudes, or are they being wise by waiting until marriage? Consider some data on the trend of living together before marriage:

> Contemporary studies indicate that the marital argument is not sound. Of 100 couples who cohabit, 40 break up before they marry. Of the 60 who marry, 45 divorce—leaving only 15 of 100 with a lasting marriage. Thus, cohabitation has two negative effects: it sharply reduces the number who marry, and dramatically increases the divorce rate of those who do.[2]

Indulgence seems to prove the connection between good faith and good works. But the truth is that the openness of the sexual revolution is destructive to home building. Therefore, sin appears to be destructive to the preservation of the wider culture.

Diluting Orthodoxy

There is an apocryphal tale of a sign that appeared in an English butcher shop during the bombing siege of London. Those were heavy rationing days, and meat was almost never for sale by any butcher. One butcher shop put up a sign that read: "Blended Horse, five pounds, six shillings."

A carnivorous customer asked cautiously, "What is your horse blended with?"

"Rabbit," came the reply.

"In what proportion is it blended?" asked the customer.

"Fifty-fifty," answered the butcher, "one rabbit to one horse."

I cite the secularization of the church in the paragraphs above to ask the question that lies at the center of this book: Is traditional faith, biblical faith? If so, does this mean that cultural immorality marks the current Christian era as one of evangelical irrelevance? I must add to this the further issue of the general weakening of the doctrinal substance on which modern evangelicalism is based.

Further, as the church grows soft on biblical preaching, does it complicate the hope of its own survival? Is the gelatinous doctrine of the emergent church guilty of the widening of doctrinal permissiveness? Brian McLaren encourages us to adopt a more "generous orthodoxy."[3] Whether we see this as right or wrong is beside the point. That McLaren can exert force at the center of evangelical conservatism probably says we are not where we were. And the most interesting thing about jettisoning orthodoxy is that this time it has come from the *Christianity Today* theological position.

It is possible to broaden Christianity to the point that it no longer is Christianity. Still, for the most part, evangelicals have been stingier with grace than they need to be. I am prone to say that McLaren has been far too generous with his orthodoxy and that most evangelicals have been far too stingy with it.

Frederick Faber wrote the hymn "There's a Wideness in God's Mercy" in 1861. I don't think he wrote it to widen orthodoxy but rather to shake up Christians who had grown too stingy with grace. The fifth stanza says:

But we make his love too narrow
By false limits of our own;
And we magnify his strictness
With a zeal he will not own.

I for one still miss the good old days (the 1970s) when heresy was always born in the Harvard Divinity School. In those days all of the people who tilted with the validity of the virgin birth were *Harvardites*. It was a lovely day. Hell, as evangelicals supposed, was located just beneath the study carrels of the Ivy League universities. It was comforting to know that whatever aberrance they thought up at Harvard could be successfully put down at Liberty University, the theological DMZ of northern Virginia.

This issue of biblical interpretation became almost geographical as well as philosophical at this point. Southern Christians saw New England churches as the instigator of liberalism. Dixie was where scriptural infallibility prevailed. Liberty University still practices Southern Baptist theology, which rarely examines the creeds, but it remains devoted to such lesser evidences of orthodoxy as gender and evangelism. I don't say this to put down Southern Baptists but instead to affirm that the vast majority of our 16 million members who can't define diluted orthodoxy are still holding forth their ban on women in the ministry rather than joining the Ivy League conversations on liberalizing the Apostles' Creed. In some ways it is an old argument that came on with the Reformation, but a strict allegiance to some Pauline passages has kept the issue of women in ministry at the forefront.

We also distrusted the barren, northern Ivy League, I might add. I remember when Karl Barth visited one of the Ivy League schools and there was a widely published photo of Barth and well-known theologians sipping vermouth and discussing the virgin birth. I thought to myself, "Oh pshaw! They could not be truly Christian theologians and be sipping cocktails while discussing such sacred propositions." Later I had to separate my Baptist hang-ups from my theological respect for the Apostles' Creed. The vermouth is not the point. What is the point? The general, casual attitude toward the Christology of the occasion.

Even so, the parentheses in the creeds that those earnest men and women established are now gathering a lot of accord. Everywhere one hears their cries of creedal orthodoxy under amendment: "The virgin birth—what a nightmare for genetics!" or, "On the third day he rose again? I hope you don't mean bodily!" or, "Descending into hell? Preaching to the spirits in prison? Jesus had a pulpit in Hades?"

> In short, Mr. Jefferson's Jesus, modeled on the ideals of the Enlightenment thinkers of his day, bore a striking resemblance to Jefferson himself.
>
> Marilyn Mellowes[4]

The gates are down now. Doubt anything. Revise everything. Make the faith reasonable. But this argument did not start in the twentieth century. There are two famous revisionists who preceded us by centuries. One was a theologian and one a politician.

The first was Marcion, a second-century Gnostic who moved to Rome in AD 140 and founded the Marcionites in AD 144. Marcion went through the Synoptic Gospels and made his own handwritten copies of each Gospel, omitting the miracles of Jesus. It seemed logical to Marcion, and the position flourished for a while.

The other famous revisionist was the politician and Deist, Thomas Jefferson. He began work on his book on the moral philosophy of Jesus in 1803 and then set it aside, later finishing it in 1819. His work went undiscovered until the end of the nineteenth century and then was printed for the first time. He did the same kind of work that Marcion had done in the second century, though it is unclear whether he knew of the

> Truth is not something we control or capture or tame. Truth is wild, mysterious, alive and always on the prowl to capture, confront and find us! The job of the seminary is not to explain the Bible, but to strike terror into the hearts of anyone who decides to read it.
>
> Mike Yaconelli[5]

famous, ancient Gnostic. In general, Jefferson excised the miracles, focusing on the moral teachings of Christ.

The difference between these two revisionists and modern theologians is that the current revisionists don't excise any verses.

Instead they fill the texts with what they would call "reasonable question marks" and leave them in the Bible, doing all this using the same translations the rest of us use. And since the miraculous passages they question differ even among themselves, they do not delineate which of them they most firmly hold. They may see themselves as conscientious evangelicals and within their way of thinking as religious conservatives.

But I believe there is the one grand point of agreement about their intention based on two things about the new alterations being made to the creeds: (1) I believe that those who continually amend the faith once delivered to the saints are doing it to be intellectually honest with themselves. (2) I believe they are doing it to be relevant. In other words, they smacked into the brick wall of unreasonable biblical things and declared, "We can go no further with these irrational ideas. So we are not out and out declaring them outside of the Christian faith; we are simply declaring a few parts of the creeds parenthetical." Part of the parenthesis is fact and part not fact, but ambiguities are good. The wrangling is human. The creed never should have begun, "I believe in Jesus Christ," but, "I'm thinking Jesus over . . . how about you?"

Is the wrangling good for us? Does it ultimately deepen our faith? I believe it does. Doubt and full belief take up the same amount of our cerebral cortex. When we agree to doubt anything and then walk away from it, the space it holds in our brains never gets any larger or smaller. The same can be said for unexamined belief. Doubt a thing or really believe it or consider it, and the space it requires is greater. Our brains, like our bodies, gain muscle from the exercise.

> Let us hold unswervingly to the hope we profess.
>
> Hebrews 10:23

In a myth of his own making, Dave Tomlinson reconstructs the parable of the Pharisee and the tax collector in a story designed to confront smug doctrinarians:

An evangelical speaker and a liberal bishop each sat down to read the Bible. The evangelical speaker thanked God for the precious gift of the Holy Scriptures and pledged himself once again to proclaim them faithfully. "Thank you, God," he prayed, "that I am not like this poor bishop who doesn't believe your Word and seems unable to make his mind up whether or not Christ rose from the dead."

The bishop looked puzzled as he flicked through the pages of the Bible and said, "Virgin birth, water into wine, physical resurrection. These things are hard to believe in, Lord. In fact, I'm not even sure I'm in touch with you in a personal way. But I'm going to keep on searching."

"I tell you," said Jesus, "that this liberal bishop, rather than the other man, went home justified before God. For those who think they have arrived have barely started out, but those who continue searching are closer to the destination than they realize."[6]

Maybe Tomlinson's illustration is a bit extreme; nonetheless, those whose faith has never struggled have no living faith. At the brink of our inner struggles is the place where faith is born. No brink, no faith.

I am working, however, on the issue of the dangers found in diluting our core beliefs. And for this I must ask: Who are those people who faced the brink and asked the big questions? What did they find out about the nature of God?

One of them was unquestionably Karl Barth. He was a pastor in Safenwil, Switzerland, during World War I. When the Allies aligned against Germany and the ravages of war spread their clammy fingers across Europe, he found that the liberal theology of the nineteenth century was too anemic to bring any hope to his people. He read and preached

> What needs to take place today in the interests of peace is in the first place . . . a spiritual Reformation and thus a conversion of Christians and of the Christian churches themselves—a conversion to the truth of their own message.
>
> Karl Barth, January 1963

the Bible in a new way. He wanted the Word of God with enough muscle in it to bring hope to his hopeless members. He didn't go crazy, but he began to read the Word for all he was worth.

> The Word of God, said Barth, has a three-fold form: the primary form is the *living* Word expressed in Jesus Christ; the secondary form is the *written* Word of Scripture, which testifies to the living Word; and the third form is the *proclaimed* Word, which is the church's proclamation of Christ the living Word. The three are inextricably linked together, the Word of God in Christ being primary.[7]

Barth doesn't say it, at least at this point, but the Word is the apostle John's towering definition of Christ and the Scripture's grandest metaphor of his identity.

Not diluting orthodoxy means that the Word of God must be seen as so trustworthy that to read it is to allow its fearsome work of changing us. The Bible is not a book given to us as something to talk about in our discussion clubs. The Bible is a flaming terror given to correct us, to give us courage to cover our cowardice, and to give us vitality enough to call us to stand and having done all to stand. It is a face-lift for our old sour countenance, a renovation of a life we are tired of, and a call to purpose when we cannot figure out why we were ever put on this planet. It is the only kind of truth that is in the end fearsome truth—so true that we are afraid to disobey it.

But to avoid diluting our orthodoxy, I believe it is necessary to read the Bible in a brand-new way; to not cry merely, "This Bible contains no errors," but to cry that we have found it faithful to our every need. We do not peruse its pages to seek to prove it is true. We do not search it to find out medical, scientific, or genetic truth. We need the kind of truth it offers that we can find nowhere else. We know that it is true enough to help us. And better than that, it is trustworthy. And if *trustworthy* and *inerrant* are nearly synonyms, as John Stott believes, then surely we are all inerrantists.[8]

We are the people of the Book.

We are daily made rich by the revelation of God.

But in the end, the Word is more than words; *faith* is the word made flesh in Jesus Christ.

PART 3

The Politics of Missions in the Global North

Klaus Issler has quoted an anonymous source as saying:

> After nearly nine years as missionaries, my wife and I returned to our sending church, a large church in the US in which we had been deeply involved in the life of the church in numerous leadership, board, and ministry capacities for many years. We anticipated a warm welcome by all these friends we'd left nearly a decade ago. We saw some familiar faces in the crowd but quickly realized we only knew these people as a crowd; the sum of our church relationships was what we did in groups.
>
> How different from our experience on the mission field. We were frequently in one another's homes. Our ministry was more one-on-one and deeply personal. It didn't take long to discover that our connection to that group overseas was deeper and stronger because we knew the stories of individuals within the group. We had personal friendships that went deeper than anything we'd ever experienced

in America. Leaving that group was gut-wrenching because of the life connections we had with the individuals within the group.

Our sending church now felt unfriendly and impenetrable; conversations superficial and deeply unsatisfying. We noticed that people would come and go within the group without anyone noticing their absence. We found ourselves dealing again with committees according to policies, procedures and protocol, not individual needs and situations.

After several weeks of frustration, we left that church and began attending a smaller church. Each week people introduced themselves to us, asked us questions about ourselves and drew us in with their genuine care—it was overwhelming. . . . We have genuine relationships with people and not just committees or teams. As a result, we sense our community is stronger, our fellowship deeper, our commitment more lasting than ever.[1]

5. SHORT-TERM MISSIONS AND THE SMALL COMMISSION

The Christian perspective is to see *every* land as a mission land, including our own in the sense that there is nowhere in the world where the gospel has penetrated as deeply as it was intended to penetrate. There is infidelity in the church wherever the church is found so that whether we're talking about an area of millions of people who have no contact with the gospel or whether we're talking about Western Europe, we are still talking about a missionary situation. Our concern should be to define what kind of a missionary witness we should have in various lands given the realities of these situations. It becomes our task to study the reality of any land that we would consider as an actual or a potential location for missionary activity and then ask what is the genuine Christian presence and what is genuine Christian proclamation in that context.

Howard Snyder[2]

6. CAN A SICK NARCISSISM HEAL A BROKEN WORLD?

The church is the most important institution on earth and the most corrupt institution on earth. The reason it is the most corrupt institution is that it *is* the most important institution. The church is very weak today. Weak liturgically. Weak in its preaching. We are supposed to have sixty million people trained and nurtured in the church. Tell me why sixty million people are having no impact on the culture? Why doesn't the church have any influence on art and on the intellectual community? How can sixty million born-again people, who have been trained and nurtured to be light to a dying world, have no demonstrable impact on the culture?

R. C. Sproul[3]

5

Short-Term Missions and the Small Commission

Christ is the Aperture of God. In the small opening of this one life, the clearest image of the whole can be seen. In Christ, God the infinite became finite. All the rays of truth in the universe focused through him.

Leonard Sweet and Frank Viola[1]

Missionaries are called to pay attention to the world. They are salespeople in a world of consumers who want to buy a different destiny. If our product is destiny—and that is exactly what the world is seeking—selling the kingdom should be easy and the transaction customary. But such salesmanship is a hurried art. The sales force too often exchanges products without looking into the eyes of the purchaser. And we who sell Jesus lose the best deals because we are pursuing the sale and missing the buyer. Who is the seller, the missionary, the merchant of salvation? Look! She is somewhat like the checker ringing up your groceries. When she is not ringing up your transactions, who is she?

She is someone's daughter, maybe someone's mother as well. She has a home she returns to when she hangs up her apron here, a kitchen that smells of last night's supper, a bed where she occasionally lies awake at night wrestling with her own demons and angels.

"You saved eleven dollars and six cents by shopping at Winn Dixie today," she says, looking right at you. All that is required of you is to look back. Just meet her eyes for a moment when you say "Thanks!" Sometimes that is all another person needs to know that she has been seen.[2]

A missionary can never be a missionary until he or she learns the art of looking around. To see the world and every person in it is the big requirement. To make this requirement a reality involves seeing people, and if we are sightless to their being, we are blind to our calling.

> Go ye into all the world, and don't start at the farthest point. The nearest point will do. You have but to open your front door and look on the mail carrier there, or open your back door and consider the person taking care of your lawn. In either child, the world is born and your global mission may begin.

I well remember the film *The Sixth Sense*, in which a little boy is counseled by a psychiatrist. His problem in his own words is this: "I see dead people." The dread of seeing them terrifies him, until his counselor wisely counsels that they are coming to seek his help. The doctor suggests that the next time he sees one of them that he talk to the dead person and ask what he can do for him or her. This advice turns his fear into ministry.

Something like this is what Jesus said on the Mount of Olives: "Go into all the world and talk to the dead people. Offer them life." Thus began the missions movement. Jesus saw missions as a matter of looking people in the eyes. In that first in-depth glance, a missionary is born.

The reason evangelicalism is dying is that the churches have made an unvoiced but mass decision to quit looking around. They have all agreed to die through the process of being concerned about nobody but themselves.

But you can be different. The smallest shopping trip can be global if you have your eyes open.

> The first thing we forget is what we're really trying to do. At least that's what my friend Jim Hendersen says, . . . "I'm in Home Depot . . . all I need is a *thingamajig*. Where is it and who cares? My eyes quickly scan the horizon . . . looking for a little just-in-time customer service. I want to scream: Take your eyes off those stupid boxes! Get down off that stupid ladder! Quit visiting with your coworkers! Don't pick up that phone! Pay attention to me! But it's pointless and I finally get it: I'm an interruption. An irritation. They'd prefer I wasn't in their building. They've forgotten why they went into business. . . ." Employees like these have missed the point.[3]

It is an odd conundrum that the contemporary church (and for the most part the words *contemporary* and *emergent* can be synonyms) rose from a missionary mandate. The newest cliché is using *missional* rather than *missions*. *Missional* is more a concept word, wider in meaning than its predecessor. It is generally my belief that the more a word encompasses in its definition, the weaker and less specific it becomes. Missionaries converted the heathen; that was their job description. *Heathen* is not a politically friendly word—especially if you are a heathen.

Christians who think of themselves as followers of the true God do not particularly relish the notion that Muslims consider them *infidels*. Especially in times past, it was the job description of missionaries to *convert the heathen*. In this view of things the *infidels* (Christians) were out to call the *heathen* (Muslims) to salvation. Sometimes the game got rough. Muslims put to the sword those Christians who refused to accept the true faith, and vice versa. Everybody who became a missionary *missionized*, and at the heart of missions was the concept of conversion.

But in this job to which we have all been called, we must never presume that we hold all the keys to God, that we as missionaries are the special friends of God, and that he depends on us to get all of his work done. There is a great deal of arrogance in such a presumption, and that presumption caused the people to whom missionaries took the gospel to be afraid of them. Those people often perceived that the foreigners were in their homeland not so much to give them Jesus as to wrest from them their treasure. God loves those we need to win, and he has been in their midst

> Kenyan leader Jomo Kenyatta complained that "when the missionaries came to Africa, they had the Bible and we had the land. They said, 'Let us pray.' We closed our eyes, and when we opened them, we had the Bible and they had the land."
>
> Philip Jenkins[4]

since the beginning. He doesn't need us to love the lost world, but when we attune our hearts to his, we begin to truly see.

We aren't supposed to go into the world to enrich ourselves but to enrich the poor in spirit with the Christ, who is the only source of true wealth. Unfortunately, some missionaries have focused more on the former. James Michener said this about the early missionaries to Hawaii. They went there with a spirit of abandonment, leaving all they had to serve the lost island kingdom. But within a short time, they had garnered their own private fortunes and owned the people they went to enrich with the gospel.[5]

But this much must be said: no missionaries ever followed their call without finding that God always went before them. And never have we gone alone. God is always there ahead of us. God is in the fields we have never visited, and he is waiting until we catch up. He is waiting until we join his passion, until we weep at the edge of his concern, until such time there is no mission, no missionary.

The noun *missions* has its surrounding battery of adjectives: *home, foreign,* and—after NASA—*interplanetary,* I suppose. *Foreign* is a word like *heathen.* Nobody likes to be thought of as a foreigner, probably because the homegrown antonym is *native.*

Natives belong to the land. They were born on the land; they own it. But *foreign* as an adjective implies that the foreigner is a transplanted *native*. Every foreigner is a native somewhere.

Missionaries are transplanted natives who go to a new people group as foreigners who intend to change them. Then they find themselves coping with the cold shoulder from the natives—the natives aren't all that eager to change. So their first contact with any culture often results in conflict. It is natural that our would-be converts struggle against the change we want to bring them. But as Martin Luther said in 1521, the conflict is healthy. We all resent people of passion who knock on our doors, believing they have a right to change either us or our cultural milieu.

Here's the rub: the new earmark of political correctness teaches us that no one has a right to change anyone, at any time or place, for any reason. This need to change people is seen by the politically correct as the ultimate scourge of Christian missions. Even so, both Christianity and Islam operate with a strong missionary assumption, and each of them sally forth into the world, believing that souls in the opposite camp need to be changed. Muslims believe that Christians are infidels, and Christians believe that Muslims who will not accept Christ are going to hell. Needless to say, these staid convictions on either side rankle all the would-be prospects of either faith.

> For when there is no battle for the gospel, it rusts and it finds no cause and no occasion to show its vigor and power. Therefore nothing better can befall the gospel than the world should fight it with force and cunning.
>
> Martin Luther, 1521

But foreigners don't just find themselves in hot water because they leave their own country and go somewhere to change people of other cultures to match their own ideologies. Foreigners are also forced to cope with their own adaptability. When natives decide to become foreigners, they face huge issues of cultural adjustment. How do we adjust to such stress? For our purposes here, we devise two categories of missionaries: (1) *short-term*, those who stay less than two weeks, and (2) *long-term*, those who stay longer. For both kinds of missionaries, however, there are impediments on the way back to the kind of compassion we need to bring the world to a better camp.

Short-Term Missions and Absentee Compassion

Missionaries like Mother Teresa and Amy Carmichael, who transplanted themselves into a foreign culture and never again took a furlough, are all but extinct. They answered the problem of adaptability by choosing to dress and live like natives of whatever culture they hoped to redeem. Did this all-out cultural identity help them in their efforts to change the people they felt called to redeem? Of course. As their foreign ways disappeared, the natives found them not only accessible but also alike in kind, so they were very effective in planting the message they brought with them.

As I read their books, I found a kind of delicious otherworldliness about their lives. I try in vain to reconcile the T-shirt world of Teens on Mission to Old Mexico (*Tom-Tom* for short) with the higher way of spiritual formation of great missionaries such as Amy Carmichael.

It's not that I expect all short-term missionaries to be such people of depth and formation in Christ, yet there is something lacking in their devotion that could inform them as to their clear-cut commission. My own call to service was compelled by the writings of Jim and Elisabeth Elliott. I wish such delightful and delicious devotion would surface again on any new mission field of the world.

These great missionaries were missiologists who didn't develop mission theory in a seminary missions class. Each of them was driven by a notion and definition found in his or her own practice. I first read *Life in the Spirit* back in 1983. Mother Teresa of

Calcutta had, I think on her own, developed a view of missions in which each of those she served held no form or body on their own. When she touched them with healing, she saw it as touching the body of Christ.

> My poor ones in the world's slums are like the suffering Christ. . . . In them God's Son lives and dies, and through them God shows me his true face. Prayer for me means becoming twenty-four hours a day at one with the will of Jesus. . . . Only then can we put our love for God into living action through service of Christ in the distressing disguise of the Poor.[6]

Each day airplanes leave Dixie, where I live, gorged with youth choirs or men's construction teams to *missionize* in the land to which their shiny airliner is headed. By contrast, they say that nineteenth-century missionaries left England or America with all their goods packed in their coffins. They had no intention of returning. Their view of commitment was marked like that of Celtic missionaries who left the Hebrides for a shrine hidden in the future. Their pilgrimage ended only at the grand gates of eternity, for once they left, they never returned home again.

But the short-term missionaries of today depart with their return flights already booked. Do they do some good? Yes, of course, and for this we say thank you. But do they change cultures? Not really. The most valuable thing that happens is that cultures change them. Their eyes are opened

> Today, once more, when Jesus comes among his own, his own don't know him! He comes in the rotten bodies of our poor; he comes even in the rich choked by their own riches. He comes in the loneliness of their hearts, and there is no one to love them. Jesus comes to you and me and very, very often we pass him by.
> Mother Teresa[7]

> In summing up how short-term missionaries operate, a local pastor on a mission field said that they show up and determine the war is real, but when they see the oppressive size of the battle, they pack up, throw a grenade into the crowd, and run.

79

to the wideness of the world and the kingdom of heaven. They are changed, some to the extent that they later go back as missionaries to have a longer go at compassion.

Long-term missionaries carry Bibles; short-term missionaries carry cameras. The differences between the two have long intrigued and baffled me. Would I stop the short-term missionaries from going? No. But I would if I could divert the huge amount of resources they draw into their well-meaning efforts into long-term financing for the veterans who live there and come to welcome them at the airport. Their service is conditioned by their belief that the world is better because of any missionaries— long- or short-term.

> Roland Allen, in *The Spontaneous Expansion of the Church*, observed that the churches of China seemed to flourish whenever the missionaries were forced to leave. He concluded that the church of Jesus Christ has within her the capacity for spontaneous expansion, and that is what happens naturally when the church is healthy and vibrant.
>
> Erwin Raphael McManus[8]

The real truth, however, is that missions, as in China for instance, actually grew by leaps and bounds after all missionaries were barred from their land. I came to this conclusion when missionaries told me, "Go home and tell them that to observe real impact, they should cancel their five-star-hotel missions trips and send us the money to use for the meat and potatoes we need to impact the world we were called to live in year after year."

Most of the money poured into short-term missions still comes from old-line denominational churches. In centuries past, denominational churches were missionary machines. They forged spearheads into distant and difficult worlds. And they built stuff: churches to begin with, but they also built schools and hospitals, clinics and orphanages. But as their numbers have declined, so have cooperative mission funds, forcing missionaries to rely on nondenominational, local American churches to be more proactive in supporting the work in other countries. There has been a bit of indigenous, long-term thinking here, but far more short-term commitment.

I want to give the old-line denominations their due here. For to be honest, in all my travels abroad I have scarcely seen any independent, megachurch missions in comparison with huge numbers of hospitals, orphanages, and churches started by old-line denominational missionaries. My own denomination has inspired me to the point of bliss. It has indeed done much to bring the world to Christ, and on sabbaticals I have served for many months to help with this divine compulsion. Even so, my own service has been too little and too infrequent to be of any real help.

> For two thousand years Jesus has commanded us to go and make disciples of all nations. We have, at best, given this commandment nominal adherence.
>
> Erwin Raphael McManus[9]

But there is a lot that old-line denominational churches do and never get the credit. My son worked for twelve years in the Philippines. He saw that there were lots of hungry people. He got the women in his Filipino church to help him cook and distribute rice on Tuesdays and Thursdays. It was but a little dent in world hunger, but the money—sparse as it was—was provided by Christian friends, largely from two Southern Baptist churches, who believed in his work and helped finance his ministry. He spent many years there without a furlough; in his mind, what he went there to do was too vast to leave to a youth group on a mission trip. It would have been wonderful indeed if some churches had kept their two-week missionary ventures in the vault of real sacrifice and simply sent him the money to support his work.

The Changing Definition of the *Small* Commission

It has long been said there is no difference between an atheist who says, "There is no God!" and a Christian who lives it out while affirming verbally that there is one. In *The Jesus Manifesto*, Leonard Sweet and Frank Viola pose a hard-to-bear idea: evangelicals have unwittingly redefined their mission, and it is now nothing more than the church making Christ more visible in a world too dark to see him otherwise.

> We believe that the major disease of today's church is JDD: Jesus Deficit Disorder. The person of Jesus has become increasingly politically incorrect and is being replaced by the language of "justice," "morality," "values," and "leadership principles." The world likes Jesus; they just don't like the church. But increasingly the church likes the church, yet it doesn't like Jesus. . . . When we dethrone Jesus Christ from His rightful place, we tarnish the face of Christianity and redefine it out of existence.[10]

I suppose I have lived all my life under this double bind of loving the arts and loving God. But I must be honest: it is my calling in Christ, I know, that has furnished me the balance I need to go on serving with any real sense of authenticity. Though his commitment to Christ may lack the clarity we would like it to have, I still think Albert Schweitzer furnishes me a great sense of equilibrium: loving the ministry of his clinic and writing his organ compositions using the top of a trunk as though it were a keyboard. He loved music, he loved God, and thus I suppose a trunk had to serve as an organ until his clinic had bandaged the wounded God put in his way.

I was in Calcutta fifteen years ago, staying at a two-star hotel (it's amazing what kind of room you can buy if you're willing to subtract the stars from their billing). Every morning across the street from my hotel, a white van pulled up with a United Methodist cross and flame logo on the side. The missionaries burst out of that van and lugged out two huge cauldrons of rice and a bale of chopped banana leaves. By the time they arrived each morning, a long line of Indians had formed, starting a mile back into the distance. Then began an odd ritual of putting a clump of hot steamed rice onto a fragment of a banana leaf, and the poor nodded a thank you and risked burning their fingers to dip out the rice and hungrily gobble it down. All too soon the line was gone, the empty cauldrons were thrown back into the United Methodist van, and the pageant came to a close.

On each of those mornings the words of Christ swam all about me: "Inasmuch as you did it to one of the least of these My brethren, you did it to me" (Matt. 25:45 KJV). I suppose the question is this: Was the Methodists' distribution of rice really valid? It is easy to fill up a van with rice. We are tempted to say, "Who are they kidding? They're nothing more than a bunch of social gospel freaks. To feed people's bodies and let their souls perish in hell is hardly doing anything worthy."

But to be critical of those who feed the hungry in the name of Christ is a woeful sin. World hunger is real. World poverty is real. Carolina Maria de Jesus was a small, poor woman who lived in a *favela* (slum) in Sao Paulo, Brazil, making her living by picking up trash in the park. But she saved the big pieces of paper she picked up and allegedly wrote a book on those scraps that became known as *Child of the Dark*. It was not a missions book, but it placed at the front of my mind images of the other half of the 6 billion people with whom I share the planet. She had a child about the age of my own when I read her book, and it fixed in my heart the sin of my own insensitivity.

I wonder how such shortsightedness would stand up against Jesus feeding the five thousand. Why did he not witness to them instead of merely feeding them? Maybe because the best way to say that God

> While I was in Calcutta, Mother Teresa died, and I went to view her body as she lay under the flag of India in the Church of St. Thomas. My encounter with her soul seemed to be all around me in the atmosphere.
>
> I feel a conscious hold of the Holy Spirit when I watch missionaries like her actually live out the theme of their life. It is glorious and at the same time a kind of *life call* to be sure I am committed to Christ for whatever he has for me to do in the world.

is real is to say it after the stomach cramps of malnutrition have gone away so people's ears can hear. Jesus let the Methodists I saw in Calcutta speak with clumps of rice on banana leaves. It's amazing how hunger and hearing work inversely. The Southern Baptist's greatest missionary, Lottie Moon, starved to death, proving—if only to herself—that her Chinese brothers and sisters improved their hearing because she gave them her income. They bought rice with her money while she starved. But their hearing was splendid.

> Carolina Maria de Jesus often dreamed that she was a grand lady in a beautiful gown with diamonds shining in her black hair. Only the acrid odor of the slums called her back to the reality. It was then that her elegant gown turned back to rags and the only thing shining in her hair were lice.[11]

It is easy to see why the word *missional* has grown in popularity over its earlier form, *mission*. It may not keep people out of hell merely to give them bread and fish, but surely it spreads light on the pathway into heaven. I believe Viola and Sweet are correct when they say,

> We must never avoid social issues. But the distinctive mark of a Christian is that you don't begin with a social or moral issue. You begin with God. . . . If we start with the social and political as our reference point, the social gospel becomes very much social and very little gospel. In truth there is no gospel that is not a social gospel.[12]

I found myself alone on a train platform in Agra, India. It is always hot in that part of India, and I often found myself resenting the heat. Like most rich Westerners, I sometimes found myself buying a cup of anything cold to devour while I stood around resenting the heat. That particular day I bought a little six-ounce tub of strawberry ice cream to spoon over my resentment. The hungry and the poor are everywhere in India, but you can never quite see them until you pop the seal on a cup of ice cream. That day when I pulled the paper cap from the cup, just the tiniest rush of air into the vacuum container was enough to signal it to what seemed like hundreds of children. As I stuck the wooden spoon into the cup, I was aware of a sea of brown eyes all looking at me, some of them reaching out toward me, pleadingly. One particularly beautiful little boy's plea could not be ignored. But when I reached toward him extending the cup of strawberry ice cream, a score of little brown arms reached farther and faster than his. I was determined he should have it, so I placed myself between the other children and this particular little boy. And using my body as a kind of human dam, I handed him the cup.

Then a fight nearly erupted. All of them turned on the lucky little boy who held the prize, reaching as if to tear the cup of ice cream from him. But he was not to be outdone. In but a moment, and in one giant leap, he vaulted into the arms of his mother, settling his little brown legs into her filthy sari. He was safe, and so was the ice cream. Then it happened: those large brown eyes fell on me and seemed to say, "Thank you, mister!" I smiled because I knew what his eyes really said: "There is only one kind of gospel—the social gospel."

I'm quite sure that a cup of ice cream on a muggy day in India does not equal salvation. But it said to me that if I could work my will, that little boy would hold the grand prize as Jesus intended it to be offered. Jesus was, to be sure, a human being. He came in the flesh to try out his messiahship. God understood that unless salvation works bodily, it doesn't work at all. No wonder that concerning Jesus, Barbara Brown Taylor exulted in discovering in a hymn the line: "Good is the flesh that the Word has become."[13] Perhaps this is the best definition of *missional* as well.

Compassion is a word that literally means "with suffering" in Latin. The Scriptures say eight different times that Jesus was moved with compassion. He suffered with the suffering; his flesh was the monitor of all that was going on in the people's flesh. Do you understand now the phrase, "Good is the flesh that the Word has become"? I understand that the great flaw in our eroding missiology is that we are no longer moved with compassion as Jesus was. We can never call ourselves *incarnational* because Jesus does not live in us. "Bad is the flesh in which the Word does not live." Such *Word-less* disciples never see any children on crowded railway platforms. They are completely invisible to Christians who are so full of themselves that there is no room for Christ. They lack the missional understanding that the best of even small, good deeds light the path to salvation.

I was struck that when Mother Teresa died there were huge billboards all over the city of Calcutta that said, "We love you, Mother!" What would make 6 million Hindus pay such tribute to a small, Catholic nun? Had she led them all to Christ? No, only toward Christ. But for those who did reach out to Christ, all found the door to his eternity.

Can the wealthy churches of America ever make their way back to their lost passion? I doubt it. Some say the pendulum will swing back some day. But we've been there. We've expunged that falsehood. The work of historian Arnold Toynbee has convinced me that there are no pendulums in the behavior of civilizations. There have been twenty-eight civilizations that have come and gone, and none of them ever swung back to the healthy attitudes toward former values, creeds, or patriotism. They moved from birth to death. Once a civilization died, another government came and built on its land; none of the empires survived by catching the pendulum back to better health and former vitality.

> We seem to have replaced the old Cartesian axiom, "I think therefore I am," with a new one, "I shop therefore I am."[14]

It is sheer hubris that makes us believe Americans are different than Romans or Greeks or Egyptians in the matter. Bet on it. There are no pendulums. When we evangelicals leave the passion we gave to missions and replace it with a new lust for having and spending, we cannibalize our own hearts. "Materialism is the new religion of the West, if one defines religion as anything that consumes most of our time, thought and money. Some would go so far as to say that materialism is our religion. Transnational corporations are our high priests, and consumerism, our liturgy."[15] Because missions and evangelism are the bedrock of evangelicalism, to abandon our missional drive while treasuring our stock portfolios is a death wish. It is—to keep things tied to the title of this book—to cross the edge of relevance. It is to vanish.

6

Can a Sick Narcissism Heal a Broken World?

> In an age of diminished expectations, the Protestant
> virtues no longer excite enthusiasm.
>
> Christopher Lasch[1]

I have often wondered if Christopher Lasch would have called the American suburbs a *mirror world*. Narcissus-inspired, suburbanites have few great dreams. They want to survive, and even more, to thrive. They want their children to be nice but above all to be rich. They want their kids to take charge of their reasonable empires. Sex, like breakfast, is required; and who would want a life without it? Pfizer has given us Viagra, so no one needs to be impotent. Impotence is deadness. The goggle-eyed procreators, however, want to be discreet. Chemical potency must come in an unmarked envelope, delivered by a postman who winks when he drops it off.

From our wilderness of lounge-lizard joggers, is it reasonable to expect much of a missionary passion to arise? Missionaries are only remembered as those quaint souls who had sex in unimaginative ways and always under the sheets. How do I know that Narcissus is a suburban?

> Narcissism represents the psychological dimension of this dependence. Notwithstanding his occasional illusions of omnipotence, the narcissist depends on others to validate his self-esteem. He cannot live without an admiring audience. His apparent freedom from family ties and institutional constraints does not free him to stand alone or to glory in his individuality. On the contrary it contributes to his insecurity, which he can overcome only by seeing his "grandiose self" reflected in the attentions of others, or by attaching himself to those who radiate celebrity, power and charisma. For the narcissist the world is a mirror, whereas the rugged individualist saw it as an empty wilderness to be shaped to his own design.[2]

The suburban man-cave has risen in which the primeval executive arrives home to his Budweiser-stocked refrigerator and prepares for a weekend of watching basketball or football, depending on the season. The cave contains an exercise bicycle and some copies of *Men's Health* magazine so he can cycle as he catches up on what his sex life should be like. His grandparents taught him he should go to church, so he does—if it's raining. He made Bs and Cs while studying for his degree, where he graduated 317th in his class. His affections are for Jesus, of course, in a minimal way. He sees the video announcements about the upcoming mission trip to Mauritania, but those trips are always during the fall when it's important to keep up on who's at the top of the NFL—and who can even spell Mauritania anyway?

Suburbia, the mirror-land, is beautiful to drive through, but underneath her hedges and wide lawns, there is a world of hurt, abuse, and addictions, divorce and cohabitation, and psychiatry. These are the prices we pay to live in the magic world of pretense and reflection. Survival exacts a high price in mirror-land. But its greatest affliction is that it is the breeding ground of self-love and the burial ground of worldwide passion.

The worst thing about owning a lot of stuff is that with the pursuit of wealth comes the real chase: the good life. But the chase soon reverses itself. The life of treasure we seek all too soon seeks us. The having of treasure becomes the pursuer. Then materialism owns everything, and materialism is so much a this-world focus that the globe shrinks to the very small world of singular appetites and involvements. Hence we fall asleep as a Christian in a wide bed, and we wake up a Narcissus.

> It will be increasingly difficult to convince the unchurched . . . that our faith is pertinent to the 21st century if the tools of our trade are from the last century.
>
> George Barna, *The Frog in the Kettle*[3]

I spent my early years as a Southern Baptist home missionary. I lived up to my name and calling. It was my job to *win the lost*. Most of the lost I won didn't mind being won to Jesus. Almost everyone likes Jesus and is generally eager to be his friend. I gave myself to building a large church in the 1970s and '80s. As George Barna once said, I was trying to build tomorrow's church with yesterday's tools. Nobody in Nebraska really wanted to be a *Southern* Baptist. For people raised in the West or Midwest, that name seemed too geographical to be very inclusive. So I tried to tell them that as nearly as I could tell, Jesus was quite close to being a Southern Baptist—and he lived in Nazareth, not Nashville. Eventually I helped them overcome their antipathy to all the denominational adjectives, and the church became a fairly large congregation.

Even so, this congregation was built in the 1970s and '80s, during the Hybels era when the way we did it wasn't the way to do it. The church planting methodology was changing; the megachurch era was entering the birth canal. What wasn't obvious to me was that the era of evangelical decline had already begun. It wasn't easy to see it. Everybody was talking about being *born again*. Movie stars and concert artists were talking like they had just spent a month with Billy Graham, whose popularity seemed for the moment to be eclipsing Elizabeth Taylor's. But denominational growth was already flagging, even as the onset of the large-church trend was moving in.

I had not been at the task of planting a church very long before I discovered that the world had become *postdenominational*. I was so busy evangelizing souls one at a time that the term had slipped past me.

It was only when I fully understood that to be a Southern Baptist was not a label of great consequence that I also noticed that the term meant far less to them than it did to me. This postdenominational attitude has made the world ready for the *age of the megachurch*. Dr. Scott Thumma of the Hartford Institute of Religion Research wrote:

> At its most descriptive level, a megachurch is a congregation which has two thousand or more worship attenders in a week. However, size alone is an insufficient characterization of this distinctive religious reality. The megachurch is a new structural and spiritual organization unlike any other. In order to understand fully the dynamics of megachurches, they must be seen as a collective social phenomenon rather than as individual anomalous moments of spectacular growth or unique successful spiritual entrepreneurial ventures.[4]

Just how postdenominational are we? We can probably answer this question best by pointing out two impediments to globalizing missions.

1. Big Church Pride and Our Evangelistic Mandate

This could never have happened in our parents' generation when denominationalism was in the ascendency. Lutherans and Baptists knew why they were Lutherans and Baptists. The categories were worth fighting for, and most of their differences were cherished for their right to hold separatist viewpoints. Most of the time they were congenial as they joshed each other, elbow to rib cage. Baptists immersed people in water, while Methodists "dry-cleaned." Episcopalians got a fifth for the Fourth, while Baptists gluttonized at potlucks. Methodist Sunday schools ran promotions in the fall, while Lutherans celebrated Oktoberfest.

As we moved into postdenominationalism, we also modified our missions emphasis. As our missions focus increasingly became busy setting up trips and raising money, it became difficult to *do* missions. In changing its focus, missions has lost its pietistic heart. I credit this infamous substitution of *pietism* for a shallow *busy-ism* with the change from true *missionaryism* into a T-shirt replica that forms prayer circles in airport lobbies but in all honesty exhibits too little long-term love and affection.

Why did we do this? Because we mistook ardor for depth. Viola and Sweet put in words what should have been our motivation: "To our minds, there is one reason why a Christian would not be absolutely occupied and consumed with Christ. That person's eyes have not been occupied to see his greatness."[5] They go on to point out that while Christ is preached regularly in our churches, he comes across as small and uncaptivating because those who preach him are not involved with him in any serious way.

Besides our loss of real Christ involvement, we have also become quite impressed with ourselves. We like being sophisticated and arrogant. I well remember one woman who came to my church after moving to our city. She said she had read my books for years and cherished them because she thought she knew who I was. When she saw my name on the church marquee, she was overwhelmed. "Since you were so brilliant, I thought you were dead. Most brilliant writers are dead, you know," she said. I told her that I hated to disappoint her, but I actually prefer being alive, no matter how much it diminished my reputation in her eyes. Then she said candidly, "I also thought you were a Presbyterian. Most brilliant writers are, you know." Once again I told her I was sorry to disappoint her by being more low-brow in my choice of denominations, but I had no desire to step up to respectability by changing denominations.

Years ago, Vance Packard wrote a piece on denominational status that focused on the long road from Pentecostalism to Episcopalianism. The denomination most respected in those days was the Episcopal denomination, and Episcopalians had a penchant for reminding the less favored that they had supplied the nation with at least eight presidents. At this braggadocio, Pentecostals blushed at their own political impoverishments. Baptists had at least four, none of whom were terribly notable, and after Bill Clinton's inglorious escapades, they generally quit counting. Presbyterians ranked higher than Methodists, who ranked higher than Baptists, who ranked higher than Catholics, even after John Kennedy. But all this religious snobbery fell away in the last few decades as the soaring triumphalism of megachurch pastors caused people to quit counting Episcopal presidents.

Rick Warren, who has sometimes been called the *national pastor*, is a Southern Baptist. Max Lucado, the Church of Christ leader, also held the title for a while. Joel Osteen was next.

Originally, denominational congregations came to be under the old nomenclature. We believed in *missions* and *evangelism*. In short, we defined our task as communal, and we spoke of *soul winning* and *foreign missions*.

I began teaching in a seminary just as the new nomenclature was being born. The word *missions* was replaced by *missional*, which is so much broader. You are missional only if you serve the Matthew 28:18–20 text and think of all fund-raising activities as missional. Car washes, rummage sales, local dental or medical clinics—all now are called *missional*.

The endless list of missional activities seems to have come at the cost of a loss of passion for the actual *winning of souls* to Christ. Currently the more cerebral disciple makers see the disappearance of many flimflam gimmicks—the Four Spiritual Laws, witnessing bead bracelets, the Roman Road to Salvation, the Navigator Bridge—and they say, "Good riddance!" But while we have willingly given up the junky methodology, we also seem to have lost a sense of the passion of it all. We have forgotten that Pentecost was a matter of fire, and it came only to those who let Christ have the final say in everything. The followers of Christ quit preaching and started talking. They traded zeal for conversation; they traded burning for meditation. I miss seeing the spontaneity of joy, the glorious testimony of those who came out of lives of abuse, addictions, and broken marriages, and the delight of those whose broken lives have been restored. A new propriety came to take its place. It is more controlled and more reasonable. But it is also passionless. Worse than all this, it left the possible involvement of the Spirit outside the experience of the worshiper.

> By means of his one Spirit, we all said good-bye to our partial and piecemeal lives. We each used to independently call our own shots, but then we entered into a large and integrated life in which *he* has the final say in everything.
>
> 1 Corinthians 12:13 Message

Propriety is the result of programming, sometimes ultraheavy programming. We start our dull services with countdown clocks to make sure the ennui is born at straight-up eleven—if it can't be purposeful, it's at least nice to see it start on time. We schedule our eighteen-minute sermons, which are punctuated with more humor than exposition, so they don't take any more digits from the digital clock than necessary. Everything moves and stops according to schedule. The Holy Spirit hovers around looking for a place to land, and alas, finding no runway for his involvement, often decides to leave worship to the staff, who, though wildly creative, plod their way clear through until noon on Sunday.

2. It's Not East versus West Any Longer; It's North versus South

Having wrangled through this earlier, let us admit that at the heart of the gospel lie two very politically incorrect assumptions: (1) not all religions are the same, and (2) the only way to get into heaven is to make Christ the Lord of your life. I cringe each time I say this, but I would cringe even more if I denied it. No, I cannot deny it. I am all bound up in Christ, and to deny him is to wipe out my existence with a lie.

In 2002 Philip Jenkins's *The Next Christendom* fell like a bombshell on our drowsy missiology. I was at first very excited about the book and his unbeatable philosophy and definition of healthy missions:

> We are currently living through one of the transforming moments in the history of religion worldwide. Over the past five centuries or so, the story of Christianity has been inextricably bound up with that of Europe and European-derived civilizations overseas, above all in North America. Until recently, the overwhelming majority of Christians have lived in White nations, allowing theorists to speak smugly, arrogantly, of "European Christian" civilization. Conversely, radical writers have seen Christianity as an ideological arm of Western imperialism. . . . Over the past century, however, the center of gravity in the Christian world has shifted inexorably southward, to Africa, Asia, and Latin America. . . . "the centers of the Church's universality are no longer in Geneva, Rome, Athens, Paris, London, New York but Kinshasa, Buenos Aires, Addis Ababa, and Manila." . . . This trend will continue apace in coming years. . . . Christianity should enjoy a worldwide boom in the new century, but the vast majority of believers will be neither white nor European, nor Euro-American.[6]

Still, those who see skin color as the only difference between American Christians and African Christians need to see things

96

as they really are. John Shelby Spong, the famous—if not infamous—bishop of Newark, declared that even the Anglican bishops of Africa were holding on to a kind of animism and practicing a very superstitious form of Christianity. Spong went on to say that African Christianity was a "thinly disguised continuation of ancient paganism, with all its unenlightened moral trappings."[7] This amalgam is highly syncretized, and the process is not over yet. Jesus and the holy family often come across as tribal gods.

Jenkins never tries to gloss over the animistic tone of some African religious passions. It is still a land where witches are systematically and regularly sought out and burned. Polygamy abounds (as it always has) and is accepted—most missionaries refuse to address it in order to make Christianity more acceptable than its North European, monogamous base would have it be. In one Jesus-centered witch raid, more than a thousand witches were hacked to death. Of course we must acknowledge that many of the more enlightened cultures were big on killing witches, and the Reformed theologians of Massachusetts Bay once took their turn at it as well. But in all fairness to the New Englanders, they never held a candle to the Christians of Zaire in the scope of their witch hacking.

> Even today, a single outbreak of witch-panic can lead to hundreds of murders in a period of weeks or months. Moreover, one of the main centers of modern witch-hunting activity has been South Africa, the most developed state on the whole continent.
>
> Philip Jenkins[8]

The encumbrances of tribal life on anything resembling biblical Christianity are too many to imagine. Nor does the idea of biblical authority, so popular in the Reformation and following, exert any control on the vast marriage of tribal paganisms and Pauline theology. But consider this: if the early Christian missions moving across Scotland and Ireland picked up Easter (named after Eostre, a Celtic goddess of fertility) and married bunnies to the resurrection, what could happen in Africa, with its stick gods, devils, and

97

black magic—especially in the light of a modernized and baseless contemporary Christianity in the global North?

Christianity will soon be caught up between a voiceless protest of cohabitation and free sex and the abusive, polygamous sexuality of the global South. I was chagrined, as were most people who really listened, by the Broadway musical the *Book of Mormon*, which studies Ugandan missionary morality and swallows it up in tribal sexuality. The implications are all there as to how far the final syncretism may actually go. But we ought always to measure this: no people were ever missionized without pulling into the faith as much as it ever sent out from the faith.

The message of Christian missions has already been weakened by secularism in the global North. We have pulled in a new secular Christian style, hatched more in Las Vegas than on Olivet. The result has been a weakening of the faith and a smug contentment that cares increasingly less about missions. I suspect that when most future Christians hear the call, "Go ye into all the world," the confused reply will be, "And exactly where would that be, dearie, and what difference would that make?" It's a fair question; it deserves a vital answer.

Before we go out to heal, we need to check our own health. A cankered missiology does not have much to offer a world in need of healing.

PART 4

The Dull Information Age

Because of what computers commonly do, they place an inordinate emphasis on the technical process of communication and offer very little in the way of substance . . . the computer is almost all process. There are, for example, no "great computers," as there are great writers, painters or musicians. . . .

When the Dallas Cowboys were consistently winning football championships, their success was attributed to the fact that computers were used to evaluate and select team members. During the past several years, when Dallas has been hard put to win more than a few games, not much has been said about the computers, perhaps because these people have realized that computers have nothing to do with winning football games and never did. One might say the same about writing lucid, economical, stylish prose which has nothing to do with word processors. Although my students don't believe it, it is actually possible to write well without a processor and, I should say, to write poorly with one.

Neil Postman[1]

7. THE FLAT-EARTH EVANGELICAL

The iConfess application for the iPhone was released a year
ago by a US company, www.littleiapps.com. In a *USA Today*
article, Cathy Lynn Grossman writes that it "has been down-
loaded more than 100,000 times. Sacraments can't be done
virtually so 'you are not YouTube-ing or e-mailing your confession,' says Patrick Leinen, a cofounder of the company.
The app is a 'personalized examination of conscience,' an
aid that prompts you through the required pre-confession
soul searching. Then you can bring your notes right in to
meet the priest."[2]

8. THE COMPUTER AGE AND THE LOSS OF INTIMACY AND MYSTERY

The old communication formula for persuasive speech
comes in zones, chalked off in feet and inches:

- 12 to 20 feet is the public distance. This is the distance
  at which we make speeches, direct traffic, teach and
  share information. . . .
- 0 to 18 inches is the intimate distance. This is the distance at which we propose marriage, agree to hear
  and keep secrets and welcome others into our intimate
  circles of friendship and trust.

Preaching occurs at all these distances, but life-changing
commitments occur when our voices are low and we agree
to soul-bond trust and conversion. . . .

Maybe the secret to large church vitality is making a place
for the intimate distance. Maybe in the long run, this is what
makes a place for true passion and lasting change in the
human heart. Maybe not everything can be big even in big
churches. Maybe it's the stuff—that whispered stuff—that
gives the blare of grace a right to its own small whispered
celebrations. Maybe there are places where the Jumbotrons
should just sit it out as quiet things are bringing the world
before God.[3]

7

The Flat-Earth Evangelical

The imagination is fed primarily by words and concepts, not by visual images. When we watch images, the messages they convey tend to bypass our thinking and influence us subjectively in ways we may not comprehend. But when we hear words, we can create our own images in our imagination; and these images are more meaningful to us than the ones manufactured by the media experts.

Warren Wiersbe[1]

Barbara Tuchman, the brilliant Yale historian, twice won the Pulitzer Prize for her philosophical histories, *The Guns of August* and *Stilwell and the American Experience in China, 1911–45*. She also won the US National Book Award in History for *A Distant Mirror*—her comparison of the calamitous fourteenth century to the twentieth century. She likened the exploding information of both eras to similar events.[2]

The computer in our day was presaged by the printing press in the fifteenth century. It may have been a happy day when those first inventors started tinkering around in their garage and came up with a primitive computer, but think of the tinkering that Gutenberg did in his garage when he jerry-rigged a winepress and came up with movable print! In each case, the world came alive with knowledge—all at once. Marshall McLuhan said the impact of the Gutenberg press and computers was very similar. Fifty years after Gutenberg's invention, there were printing presses in 110 cities, and 8 million books had been printed—all of them filled with information that had been previously unavailable.

> Gutenberg made everyone a reader. Xerox makes everyone a publisher.
>
> Marshall McLuhan[3]

> There were books on law, agriculture, politics, and exploration, metallurgy, botany, linguistics, pediatrics, and even good manners . . . so much new information, new formats, among the most important innovations being the use of Arabic numerals to number pages. . . . Pagination led to more accurate indexing, annotations and cross referencing.[4]

The first known example of the use of page numbering was the New Testament Luther translated into German in 1522. Ultimately that and the numbering of Bible chapters and verses led to a vastly more useable Bible.

Digital, Dot-Com, Dull

What has all of this to do with the decline of evangelicalism? The dominance of the computer became so overwhelming that the digital world forced the religious world under the spell of its influence. The computer eventually dominated every area of parish and doctrinal importance. The sermons and programs of the church were easily approached and controlled by the keyboard and mouse. But did it make the programs more personal or the sermons more interesting?

Five hundred years after the invention of the printing press, what has computer technology done for us? As Thomas Friedman says, the once-round world grew a little flatter. What became of all the information? It just lay out there waiting for someone to find it. It may have caused some excitement when a junior high school student became curious and brought up WikiLeaks; but in general the world continued to grow flatter, and nowhere was creativity more eliminated and wiped out than in churches. And what is so unusual about it is that each of these contemporary churches felt they were unique and never stopped to realize that almost none of them actually were. The church was much better attended with a lot more vitality before the computer arrived on the scene. What would be truly unique is if someone suddenly found the Holy Spirit active in their midst.

Thomas Friedman looks at the computerized generation quite honestly in *The World Is Flat*. The computerization of the world has landed not with a creative effect, says Friedman, but with a dull sameness. Corporations are not as unique as they suppose; they actually are extremely boring in their electronic coincidence.[5] What Friedman says of corporations is true also of American evangelicalism.

This wide world of possibilities has been narrowed down to braggadocious, look-alike websites that glare on internet screens coast to coast. But the dimensions of the world are wider than that. McLuhan says the computer merges all the hemispheres into a single, connected ball. The evangelical begins to vanish because the digital congestion leaves people less important than the communication syndrome it sponsors. The media gospelizers and the megachurch pastors all come across with a common electronic grin that looks out over the dot-com world and says, "Welcome! Here's our menu!"

The menu, however, is remarkably unremarkable even though it promises unique, creative worship that is true to the Bible and is full of promos that focus on all they are going to do for you if you attend. They all have audiovisual teams who can animate their way into your life with the latest electronic goo-gaws set to grab your interest. They all have something good to say about the Bible and Jesus and how he can change your life. They run a couple of testimonials of adherents who have come to the worship center and found their lives remade. Evangelicals gradually vanish from church—because the church has moved into their homes.

> The new electronic interdependence recreates the world in the image of a global village.
> Marshall McLuhan[6]

I recently pulled up the Facebook page of the pastor of one of the megachurch giants on the West Coast. Typically, he is dressed in torn Levis and a baseball cap, and the hit counter says he has 160,000 hits a week and has more Facebook friends than Abraham's descendants. Most of my Facebook friends seem to have upward of a thousand friends, while I feel darn lucky to have forty-five. But I have a feeling that the people out looking for more friends are doing so in order to keep improving their self-image, and when I check their Facebook page or blog, I can see that they have truly *had their socks blessed off* for being so unique. I wear tighter socks, and it takes quite a shaking to dislodge mine. Again, I am not so moved by how unique each of these evangelical moguls are but by how very similar they are. The evangelical world is flat, and we are vanishing partly because its flatness is universally dull and uninteresting.

But it isn't just their websites that leave this impression. Their worship services are also flat. The digitized worship leaves people saying, "I've heard this all before in the very same way." Copycat worship styles and copycat sermons leave all evangelicals so similar that there is little difference among churches and preachers. Dropping out is an easy thing to do once you think you know everything that's been said and the way it's been said. They all start with the Jumbotron clock I referred to in the last chapter. This digital worship minder, like a NASA countdown, number the minutes and seconds I have to wait for the launch of the explosively creative service to begin. At the end of the countdown comes blastoff. Then the 10-9-8-7 sequence ends at 0, the amps roar, the good times start, and the Jumbotrons flare to life. The songs remain the same from church to church, video short-subjects roll, and then the sermon outline—set coincidentally to match the one the ushers have put in my hand—rolls out over the audience. It's all a bit overkill, and overkill lures the bored into disinterest, and the disinterest leads to decline.

The digital clock is far removed from early clocks, which Lewis Mumford viewed as the key invention of the Industrial Revolution. The clock, paradoxically, originated in the Benedictine monasteries of the twelfth and thirteenth centuries, and it was used to regulate the seven devotional periods of the monks. A century or so later, the clocks moved out of the monasteries into the village steeples and towers to regulate the work and play (what little play there was) of the villagers, marking their lives with routines of all sorts. But the twelfth-century Benedictine monks could never imagine the computer or what would happen when the computer and the clock were united in holy wedlock.

I have been in worship planning sessions in which church staff members kept one eye on the clock and the other on the computer while planning Sunday worship. Every chorus, drama, Scripture, video, and sermon is planned down to the second. The idea is that it is a sin against the Holy Spirit to go past the last bell.

> The clock was invented by men who wanted to devote themselves more rigorously to God; it ended as the technology of greatest use to men who wished to devote themselves to the accumulation of money. In the eternal struggle between God and Mammon, the clock quite unpredictably favored the latter.
>
> Neil Postman[7]

It is probably worth mentioning, however, that the Holy Spirit is the one critical agent of worship who can't be summoned up in a dot-com fashion. And best of all, the Spirit is creative and mysterious. He can't be pixilated or cut and pasted. He charges the air in worship. He is alive, demanding, and upfront. He is so real and demanding that he makes decline impossible.

I wonder if what Neil Postman says of a techie bureaucrat may also be said of a techie contemporary churchman:

A bureaucrat armed with a computer is the unacknowledged legislator of our age, and a terrible burden to bear.

Neil Postman[8]

While I cannot prove what I am about to write, there is such authority in a computer screen that to arrive at such authority any other way seems weak. One of the children in one of my favorite movies says, "If it's in the computer, the world believes it!" Before we were into the authority of the computer, we were more clearly interested in the authority of God. Computers have arrived with their own authority to start and stop clocks at will. They also can start and stop services, no matter what the Holy Spirit may have to say about it.

One gets the feeling that any clever cleric who can get his Jumbotrons working with his PowerPoints can rule the contemporary church world. In a way it is so digitally creative that the Holy Spirit cannot compare. As the Jumbotrons have gotten bigger, the gospel invitations to salvation have gotten shorter, and in many if not most cases have been dropped altogether. One thing is for sure: sermons generally are getting ever shorter and less substantial.

The flat world of computer-driven faith is dull indeed. Does it breed dull disciples? I think so. It also breeds decline—at first in interest and then in attendance. Finally, evangelism declines and evangelicals appear to have vanished.

We would do well to remember that the computer is a machine and therefore operates mechanistically. It works its binary miracles on a mindless, mathematical configuration of ones and

Neil Postman was doubtless thinking of computers when he wrote of common thermometers:

> Machines of various kinds will sometimes assume a human or, more likely, a superhuman aspect. Perhaps the most absurd case I know of is in a remark a student of mine once made on a sultry summer day in a room without air conditioning. On being told the thermometer read ninety-eight degrees Fahrenheit, he replied, "No wonder it's so hot!"[9]

Computers only put out what we have put in. The mystery of godliness is born in the seeking heart and not the mechanics of seeking transformation in dull digits. When every church in the world has forgotten this, worship will have perished from the earth.

zeroes. Furnish your best sermon on the cross and, as far as the computer knows, it could be a treatise on cold fusion. It may also appear as a cold fusion lecture to the congregations who miss the warm heart of the book of Acts. The computer is not essential to revival or any other evidence of Pentecost. Yet we continue trying to arrive at honesty with God by pushing the numbers racket. The computer can stack the ones and zeroes in favor of interest or of program, but it cannot supply life or mystery to the strobes and smoke machines. In his letters, Paul speaks of the mysteries of the gospel twenty-one times, but never more definitively than in 1 Timothy 3:16:

> Beyond all question, the mystery from which true godliness
> springs is great:
> He appeared in the flesh,
> was vindicated by the Spirit,
> was seen by angels,
> was preached among the nations,
> was believed on in the world,
> was taken up into glory.

Put that in your Microsoft pipe and smoke it.

Dangerous Liaisons and Larceny

There is a further danger of the computer-driven lifestyle. Deep beneath the fabric of things that taint the Christ dream is the insidious lure of internet pornography. The estimates of the number of Christians who visit porn sites regularly is staggering. Some prominent evangelists have had their fall into pornography broadcast across the internet, but far beneath them are a thousand other pastors who were caught but were not prominent enough to become a national story. I have a friend who makes continual studies of

> Innumerable times students have told me they did a poor job on an essay or test because their all-powerful, all-authoritative computer broke down.

these preachers. He estimates that at least 50 percent of preachers log on at least once a month to pornographic websites. Further, he believes that 15 percent of all preachers watch far more regularly than that. It is quite likely that a pastor or staffer you know is locked in the struggle as well.

The comparative privacy of the internet has fostered a voyeur's boom in which all people, Christians included, can dip into the computerized sexual subculture as frequently as they like with little or no chance of discovery. No need to risk being seen dodging into a sleazy shop or buying a slick magazine in an airport kiosk. Now the click of a computer mouse can make it all happen, and the gratification is instant.

Internet porn is so easy to get into and so hard to get out of. Worst of all, once caught at it, the church staffer loses his or her reputation and probably his or her job if it is with youth in any of the various children's ministries of the church. Each time a good minister is caught in the grip of pornography, the kingdom dies a bit and a few more evangelicals drop out of the church, stabbed with the blade of disillusionment.

Leaving out the grand spoiler of porn voyeurism, there are far simpler but nearly as deadly consequences that derive from misusing the computer. I really would like to avoid this paragraph, but the whole truth must come out. Computer sermon broadcasts as well as YouTube and blog-site homilies have led to a new kind of sermon preparation that often results in a resurgence of homiletic theft. Some years ago in a church near my parish, an acquaintance of mine stole a Swindoll sermon and preached it word for word to the congregation the next Sunday night. It was brilliant. Unfortunately, now when any preacher delivers a brilliant sermon, it can raise suspicions—particularly if *brilliant* is not customarily applied to him.

Only a week or so after his all-star delivery, the Swindoll organization aired a replay of the stolen sermon. Some members of the congregation who heard it reported the theft without really realizing who actually was the thief. "You know," said one bewildered parishioner, "Charles Swindoll stole a great sermon our pastor preached last week. How can Swindoll call himself a man of God and go around stealing sermons from our staff? Shame! Shame!" But most of the elders saw the real truth. The thieving associate was called in and reprimanded. He was allowed to keep his position but was put on probation until his sin was atoned.

As a professor, I usually grow suspicious when a student turns in a brilliant paper or sermon when *brilliant* isn't an adjective I would usually apply to him. Students lean heavily on the internet, which can become a treasure trove of possibilities when they are

> Internet pornography provides instant gratification. Someone searching for internet porn can find it with a single one-word search on Google or Yahoo. Within minutes, a user will be deep into pornography. There is little or no time delay between the decision to engage in viewing porn and the moment it is actually found. Our culture preaches instant gratification in many areas of life and the internet makes it supremely possible.
>
> Bryant Evans[10]

behind on their assignments and it's late in the semester. Study and discipline get replaced by Yahooing, Googling, and YouTubing their way to a creative, last-minute project. But stolen academic stories are often exposed, although they cycle through academic writing so freely that it becomes hard to tell what the original source was.

I learned this truth when entering the Children's Hospital in Birmingham to make a call on a young parishioner friend. Upon entering the lobby of the hospital, my vision was captured by a huge framed poster of a children's poem called "U." It was beautifully graphic with juvenile script and illustration.

Why was I instantly drawn to it? It was one of my poems, yet nowhere was the poem attributed to me. It was quite simply a blatant example of computer theft. I told the woman attendant behind the desk that they had no right to hang my work without any hint of attribution. She told me that they didn't steal it. I sent the hospital a copy of my book in which the poem was printed and told them if they did not take the picture down, I would be forced to sue them. I don't think I would have gone that far, but my threat was enough to cause them to remove it.

The same thing happened with my book *A Requiem for Love*. After the book came out, a plagiarist retyped my published book and tried to publish it as his own. I call this sort of crime *computer delirium*—computer theft with a psychosis piled on top. Unfortunately, this sort of thing has become epidemic in our day.

As I earlier said, students have been known to copy an entire page from a reference and then turn it in as their own. Needless to say, sermons are also becoming less original. It reminds me of the story of the editor who returned a manuscript to a discouraged writer, saying, "Your manuscript is both original and good. The bad news is that the original part is not good and the good part is not original."

Decline in Biblical Authority

If the heavy fog of information has led to a flattening of creativity and to additional temptation to sin, there is yet one other way to look at what the computerized information glut has achieved. It has caused further decline in evangelicalism by weakening biblical authority. It sets forth information regarding the Bible, but with no safeguard to determine whether it is true or even reliable.

When I was a child there was a great deal of mystery that surrounded preachers. They were elite to some degree. They understood the Bible, and they opened it to us and explained deep and wonderful things. We had this book, and we had a mysterious guru who could tell us things ranging from where Cain got his wife to whatever happened to the Hittites. Nothing happened in the book that the preacher didn't understand, and he used the book to make everything fit in our questioning lives. When anyone died, he took the book and reckoned with our questions. When a baby was born, he knew why the child was under the coming supposition of original sin, and he told us.

But all of that has changed. The evangelical preacher has grown less important as an all-knowing mystic, and the Bible has gotten

> For so much of post-Reformation times the word *Bible* was the word for *book*. The medieval period was a clear example of this point.
>
> > How comforting it must have been to have a priest explain the meaning of the death of a loved one, of an accident, or of a piece of good fortune. To live in a world in which there were no random events; in which everything was, in theory, comprehensible; in which every act of nature was infused with meaning is an irreplaceable gift of theology. The role of the church in premodern Europe was to keep the deck of cards in reasonable order, which is why Cardinal Bellarmine and other prelates tried to prevent Galileo from shuffling the deck.
> >
> > Neil Postman[11]

lost in a great publishing explosion. I used to know a great many Christians who devoted their lives to Bible study. But most of the Christians I know today read novels or the constant sea of unfolding political opinion books or VIP memoirs. Needless to say, the same information explosion that is burying the Bible has also flattened Bible preaching to opinion homilies and good-feeling sermonettes that speed the congregation toward early dismissal. All this has tempted the bored evangelicals to vanish.

The computer, of course, didn't force our attention away from the Word. It's just that the lure of the one-eyed demon drew us into Facebook or the Web; and once entangled in the Web, we chose not to live in the Bible—that premodern book of mysteries and miracles. There were electronic games and Kindle books, and soon we were amazed at the flatness of the world we had created.

Conclusion

Will the day come when we will look around and find we have lost sight of the steeples that once pierced suburban landscapes? And will we realize the Christians who once attended church are gone? They vanished under a wilderness of keyboards and mice. Let us pray we will demand of our churches a way of being that will glory in vitality and life.

8

The Computer Age and the Loss of Intimacy and Mystery

The technopolist stands firm in believing that what the world needs is more information. It is like the man who complains that the food he is being served in a restaurant is inedible and that the portions are too small. . . . Attend any conference on telecommunications or computer technology, and you will be attending a celebration of innovative machinery that generates, stores and distributes more information more conveniently, at greater speeds than ever before. To the question, "What problem does the information solve?" the answer is usually, "How to generate, store and distribute more information, more conveniently, at greater speeds than ever before."

Neil Postman[1]

The information glut is not so much anti-Scripture as it is non-Scripture. The Reformation was born and matured alongside the rise of the sciences, and it was inevitable that eventually the reading world became divided in its interest. Luther and the Reformers went one way, and Galileo and his friends went another. Needless to say, the conflicts that began amiably (Galileo, Copernicus, and Kepler were all men of faith), by the middle of the nineteenth century, had become severe.

> I am informed that Mr. Galilei [Galileo] transfers mankind from the center of the universe to somewhere on the outskirts. Mr. Galilei is therefore an enemy of mankind and must be dealt with as such. Is it conceivable that God would trust this most precious fruit of His labor to a minor, frolicking star? Would He have sent His Son to such a place? How can there be people with such twisted minds that they believe what they are told by a slave of the multiplication table?
>
> Bertolt Brecht's play *Galileo*[2]

Christians are champions of their redeeming mystery. I think that for this reason, if no other, Christian apologists need to tread lightly when trying to prove the truth of Scripture empirically. I have long been urging evangelicals to develop a relational apologetic that harmonizes our opinions with our experience. Our own experiences with the God of grace live at the heart of our faith. Even if the inhabitants of the digital age doubt our faith, they are not free to doubt our testimony. If it is true for us, the technologists are not free to gainsay our personal experience with God.

After all, digital electronics can never gainsay our own experience with Christ. We Christians, and especially we preachers, are free to advance our faith on the basis of our testimonies—the stories of our pilgrimages with Christ. Our narratives are our faith.

Remember that the old communication formula for persuasive speech comes in relational zones. These zones are chalked off in feet and inches, and the best tales of our intimacy with Christ are measured in inches.[3]

- 12 to 25 feet is the *public distance*. This is the distance at which we make speeches, direct traffic, teach, and share information.

- 4 to 12 feet is the *personal distance*. This is the distance at which we socialize, sit at dinner, interact with conversation, and accept or reject counsel.

- 18 inches to 4 feet is the *private distance*. This is the distance at which we sign documents, have conversations, and decide whether we will invite the world in or take ourselves out of it.

> Stories are the tracks we leave.
>
> Salman Rushdie[4]

- 0 to 18 inches is the *intimate distance*. This is the distance at which we propose marriage, agree to hear and keep secrets, and sparingly welcome others into our intimate circles of friendship and trust.

Preaching occurs at all these distances, but life-changing commitments occur only when our voices are low and we whisper our agreement to be born again. This makes me wonder if Jumbotron worship is in some sense working against the issue of persuasion in preaching and worship. Jumbotrons always operate at the public distance, but great life decisions are made at the intimate distance.

Most megachurches these days operate their visuals at a greater distance than the movie houses do, which for the most part set their screens at no more than fifty feet from the audience. Why is this important? Because faces sell the message. People read persuasion more from the face of the persuader than from his or her arguments.

For scenes of high romance (and certainly of intimacy) in the movies, directors usually move the camera in so close that the faces of the movie stars fill the entire frame and the eyes of the actors can separate up to twenty feet apart on the movie screen. Why do directors permit such wide-screen, wide-facial close-ups? They want to bind the audience to the screen to build the intimate, emotive power of the tale they are spinning.

Television producers never do to news anchors what we do to preachers. They don't force them to stand twenty-five feet from the camera to report the news of the day. They want their faces to give us the information of the day as *talking heads*—it's what makes the evening news really work. The weakness of church Jumbotrons is that they usually don't create those kinds of close-ups. It would seem odd or too theatrical in church.

Throughout my long career of winning people to Christ, I have noticed that when I actually get down to the point of sharing the Savior, I am always very close to the person. In fact, when I ask a person to repeat the believer's prayer, my face is generally within eighteen inches of him or her. It is just a natural corollary of persuasion. In fact, I don't know if I have won anyone to Christ at the public distance; yet these days, that is the only distance at which we communicate from pulpit to pew during the sermon.

Great communication is always the work of talking to people so face-to-face that the argument of the speaker crosses all the other distances (public, personal, and private) and sets up a powerful one-on-one ratio so the audience member is convinced that the preacher is talking personally to him or her.

> To belong, to be witnessed, to be remembered, to have your life make a difference, to bless and be blessed—all have a place in your legacy.
> Rachael Freed[5]

Daniel Taylor, a man I much admire, says this kind of face-to-face talking is our legacy, particularly if we include a story in the intimate setting. This feeling of intimacy steals its way into the psyche of the hearer, and persuasion digs into the soft turf of reason to take its stand up close. These values are not electronic; they are intrinsic. They are not computer generated; they are born in reason.

But why bring up all this? Am I suggesting that all Jumbotrons be eliminated from the theater of persuasion? Not at all. Our church was one of the first in Nebraska to use Jumbotrons in the worship service. But I never appeared on camera during the sermon. We projected the hymns we were singing. (I've always been convinced people sing better once you get their faces out of the hymnal and onto the screen.) The liturgies and litanies also were projected.

Before the services began, we could project the various church programs and opportunities for service for the coming week.

But I reserved for the sermon the right to look people in the eye and try to reduce the audience (our auditorium was one of the largest in the city) to a large gathering of single conversations during which our faces were in full encounter. What has deluded us into thinking persuasion can be done in any other way? It was always impressive to see the Rose Bowl filled with people coming to Christ during a Billy Graham crusade. When the setting was right, the crusades had a Woodstock fascination about them. But in reality, most people I know who came to Christ came only at the intimate distance of persuasion.

Perhaps none of us are actually convinced that altar calls really work anymore. It is possible they are used too frequently and bring down the mood, ending a victorious service with a sense of *no-sale* failure. But this overwhelming sense of failure marks our services because people apparently have no open business to do (or that they are willing to do) with God.

Gospel invitations in these years of evangelical decline often appear to be a bit boring—or even dead. But if these gospel invitations have a place at all in church, they need to be studied and then offered when the moment is right to those who have had an eye-to-eye meeting of the minds and have sensed the rapture of loving God up close. Then Matthew 10:32 has a chance to live again in public confession; then altar decisions become more than intimate—they become tactile. We touch in prayer, kneel together, and with head-to-head togetherness we decide and then declare our commitments.

Most camera operators are sensitive enough not to turn the camera on people in the act of these encounters. Somehow what is most sacred at altars looks obscene at the public distance. Maybe we ought to bring it all down to a small circle of trust where only God and the penitent heart are welcome. Could it be that the secret to large-church vitality is to make a place for the intimate distance?

Maybe not everything can be big, even in big churches. Maybe it's the whispered stuff that gives the blare of grace a right to its own small, whispered celebrations. Maybe there are times when the Jumbotrons should be turned off to let the intimate, quiet moments bring the worshipers to God. Then and there we should surrender the logic of our preaching to issues of touch and whispers.

Hearing Bigger, Seeing Bigger

The odd electronic flattening of the evangelical world has come into worship at the head of the large-church trend. It is uncanny that the evangelical world is in decline at the very time it is pushing to grow the church. What has produced this paradox? I think the paradox was born out of a very proper zeal to win as many people as possible to Christ. There was nothing wrong with either the zeal or the dream, but the firestorm of effort had a kind of burned-over effect that ultimately acquainted everyone with the vocabulary of our mass evangelism but never seemed to improve the spiritual health of our world.

By the time this wildfire evangelism had run its course, the megachurch movement was in full sway. Their methodology was very techy—very digitally driven. The computer world of megachurch worship marched forward on such innovations as Jumbotron worship, in which amplifiers and PowerPoint graphics came to stand for the way all worship ought to be done. It was one thing to make sure the preacher was heard, but the cameras and lights created a feeling that it would be best if he was seen bigger than life.

In most churches in which the pastor appears on giant screens, the effect is somewhat bizarre. In the first place, to have giant screens in a congregation of two thousand or less is a bit of overkill. To

> I had always wondered how Jesus spoke to thousands without all the electronic goo-gaws of the computer revolution. How did they see? How did they hear? Then some years ago I was speaking to a New Mexico gathering of at least two thousand people. Just as I stood to speak, the electrical power went off because a mountain thunderstorm was raging around the auditorium. In a quandary as to what to do, I raised my voice and fairly shouted into the odd, dark silence, "What's to be done, now?" Someone shouted back from what seemed to be the last row of the auditorium, "Preach on!" And so I did, and that night I found the answer to my question of how Jesus did it. When he preached, people actually listened. There was a kind of covenant: we'll be quiet and focused, and you speak. Now, of course, with sound and image amplification, people can come or go at will. And they do. They file the word *disinterest* in their minds and leave the place, leaving their inert bodies behind.

amplify the sound has for its downside the power of letting people hear so well that they can move in and out of the sermon with no real need to pay close attention to anything. Now the magnified, projected pastor does the same thing with optics. Images are so big that an occasional glance at a twenty-foot pastor is all that is needed to make sure he is still there. The question is: Do people pay better attention to behemoth projections? I think not. Intimacy is gentle, little, and close up. It never frightens. It rarely bores.

Big churches with big projectors may fascinate for a moment, but most of us treasure the moments that do not make us afraid. We tire quickly of awe, and in the case of the megachurch, we are all too soon bored with the bigness of it and wish we were close enough to find a place in meaningful worship.

Three Events That Preceded the Rise of the Digital Church

With the introduction of mass communications, we have seen the rise of a society that is dependent on sensationalism and visual aids, numbers and notoriety. The church has followed this trend with vigor. From Billy Graham in the mid-twentieth century to the internet superstar preachers of today, the digital age has left us hungry for showmanship. The rise of the emergent church has sought to negate any moral directives from our lives, leaving us open to any and all messages that make us feel good. Evangelical Christians have grown to dismiss a person of faithfulness and moral fiber, opting instead for the latest fad and most titillating speaker. The internet and cable channels are rife with such men and women who make us feel like a million bucks but do little to help us become spiritual grownups.

1. The Loss of the Graham Ecumenism

The healthiest ecumenical earmark of the twentieth century was the rise of the Billy Graham Evangelistic Association. In 1949, a brief six years after Graham graduated from Wheaton College, he began a series of evangelistic revivals in Los Angeles. Using tents and parking lots, he held a series of three-week encounters, which spilled over into a captivating eight weeks. William Randolph Hearst, whom Graham never met in person, was nevertheless enthusiastic about the values and patriotic spirit of the young evangelist, and he ordered his chain of newspapers to promote the Graham revivals. Thus Graham's ministry was launched.

> Four out of every ten non-churchgoing Americans (37 percent) said they avoid churches because of negative past experiences in churches or with church people.
>
> Barna Newsletter[6]

His first major crusade was not to come for another ten years, but his reputation was set by the Hearst machine. All of the Graham era was fed by video and electronics as his sermons were broadcast on radio and television. The era prepared the church for the video rise of the gospel, though the computers that drove it were yet to be born. And it wasn't just the telecast that ushered in the new era. Publishing joined the effort, first with the Hearst media machine and then with magazines. This landed Graham on the cover of *Time* in 1954, and from that point on a dramatic reportage began. The major glory of the Graham years was the ecumenical spirit of the crusades. Pastors and leaders of every denomination were as taken with Graham as Hearst had been. The use of telecast and publicity came in full force.

I do not list the Graham years as the beginning of evangelical decline—certainly anything but that. But the declining enthusiasm that the crusades began to experience toward the end of the twentieth century seemed to create a waning of the ecumenical force they earlier exuded. It was also unfortunate that Graham's rise to popularity was eclipsed by the beginning of the decline in old-line denominations. In the swelling years of Graham's success, Methodists, Presbyterians, American Lutherans, and finally even Missouri Synod Lutherans and Southern Baptists (riddled by their own inner strife) contributed to the decline.

> Whether these [mega] churches actually will change the world remains to be seen. . . . The implication of this success can be seen as an unstated but real challenge to the impression that religion is impotent in a secularized society.
>
> Scott Thumma[7]

In the 1980s and '90s the era of the megachurch was born. Propelled by the digital advance, they were suddenly everywhere. Although many megachurch pastors claimed their congregation had grown by conversion growth, many fed on the dissatisfied members who were fleeing their old-line denominational churches. There are many evidences that the megachurches have not held onto their swelling memberships, for more than 50,000 new house churches have begun—in some cases taking their members from those dissatisfied even with megachurches. All in all, according to various church growth researchers, they have lost more than 12 percent of their attendance during the past decade.

2. The Rise of the Emergent Church

The postmodern emergent church movement has been a gelatinous phenomenon. Even so, it has its own prominent set of heroes. Moving away from all things traditional, they may have erred most seriously in the realm of Christology. The emergents have been reluctant to agree on any specific boundaries regarding who Jesus is and what his place is in the Godhead. Many of the young (and most of them are) pastors have antagonized the orthodox with their almost freelance thinking. Their digression from the creeds and covenants is so disturbing that it rankles members of almost all denominations. Emergents feel that the old-line denominations need to be shaken up.

I first ran into emergent church leaders at the Zondervan pastors' conference in San Diego. At the time, most of the pastors

The Nine Principles of the Emergent Church:

1. Identity with the life of Christ.
2. Transform the secular realm.
3. Live highly communal lives.
4. Welcome strangers to the community.
5. Serve with generosity.
6. Participate as producers.
7. Create as created beings.
8. Lead as a body.
9. Take part in special activities.

One cannot help but notice that as a confession of intention, this holds nothing in common with the great confessions of the church. Nothing of a faith nature really is said here, and of course, this is intentional. It allows every church to go its own way, with orthodoxy or without it. Thus the church winds up with the same conclusions as Jacques Derrida. Just as there is no truth that is true for everyone, there are no doctrines that are true for every church. It is ultimate freedom to believe or not believe, to unite or not unite, to require or not require.

were attending the conference because it was not only the largest evangelical pastors' conference but also one of the richest in terms of offering help, training, and new methodologies and programming to keep the church interesting, motivated, and growing. But the emergent leaders present were often openly antagonistic, and they often threw slurs and condescending remarks at the more traditional pastors.

The conference began to dwindle in attendance and finally disappeared (perhaps like evangelicals themselves). I don't know whether the continual disagreeable attitudes of the emergents—bellicose and outspoken to the last—caused the disappearance of the group. But it is a deep chasm that keeps widening between traditional church leaders and the emergent group.

3. Tribes and Chieftains

Along with the rise of the emergent church has come a new virtual idea from the larger world of blogs and websites. This is a widespread phenomenon of electronic togetherness called *tribes and chieftains*.

The computer generation is welcoming these pockets of togetherness, the point of which is finding your particular crowd and your own prime mover. These tribes are reflective of the tastes of both you and the people you electronically hang out with. You can make friends and build an entire life all within a few websites, momentarily checking in with your blog and Facebook world. This allows emergents to hang out electronically with other emergents, as do—to some extent—traditionalists with other traditionalists, and so on. The point is that in this electronic generation, your tribe is you. Expanding your database to include people who are so different from you that you may actually learn from them is not nearly as important as the *cozy factor*. Life should be about comfort, not the stress of working at diverse relationships. Denominations once did this. Now finding your spiritual look-alikes is a matter of locating your tribe. The Andy Stanley Catalyst tribe tends to prefer others of the Andy Stanley Catalyst tribe for their friends.

This concept originally developed from the rock concert scene, but it has widened now in every direction. Everyone lives the virtual *cozy* life before they actually indulge themselves in their kind of preferred worship experience. Then they are off on the adventure they have worked out in Starbucks lounges or bistros or casinos or whatever geographical locator their electronic tribe has agreed to meet.

Across the gamut from the secular scene are the evangelicals. Calvinist readers saturate themselves in their favorite books and Web personalities. Then they click their way around the Web until they locate someone whose tribe they would like to join. Then they choose a Facebook acquaintance, post something on his or her wall, and wait. Then the news comes in: a conference in Orlando, a coffee klatch, and the tribe begins to build. Experience, click, YouTube, click, a snuggly blog that rattles on, "feeling just the way I do," click, and a chance to vent on whatever pops up next.

When I first heard that many of the megachurch pastors were opening satellite chapels in other suburbs or cities—some quite distant from the mothership—I thought it would never work. And I am not yet convinced that it does. Now I can see, however, that a satellite chapel with the same megachurch-downloaded pastor has a better chance than I first thought. This has nothing to do with how good his sermons are or even his prowess as a great Bible scholar. It is a matter of a chieftain widening his tribe. These churches are the electronic settlements of the home village—her virtual tribe.

Can it work? For a while perhaps. The reason that it works at all is due to something very few of these megachurch chieftains will ever understand. Ernest Becker wrote of it in his Pulitzer Prize–winning book, *The Denial of Death*. In the book he postulates that people overcome their fear of death by deciding either to be a hero or to worship the right one.[8] His theory is made real by the millions of people who visit Graceland each year. If you can't be Elvis, you can gain a bit of your own ability to be remembered by just worshiping him a bit. To be fair, I know of no prominent pastors who try to promote their own idol status. Nevertheless, inadvertently they do. Each new satellite they open is an electronic altar to which laypeople can attach themselves to a chieftain, without actually moving geographically to his home.

But this virtual idolatry probably has a limit. Again, as a man who has moved beyond pendulums, I think the trend is set now. Even the electronic church cannot survive the death of the myriads of smaller churches. Remember, there are only about 1,500 megachurches in America—a small portion of the 340,000 lesser congregations. Although their leaders may never admit it, when the 340,000 smaller congregations are all gone, the 1,500 big ones will be too. The farthest reach of this doctrine of tribes is that the little tribes count too. In fact, the existence of the big mother churches is tied to the health of the little ones. When the clicking mice have run their course, the electronic church will be done for.

Conclusion

When all this has happened, the truth of Christ's promise—which will still be alive—will be realized in the ordinary issues of community, not tribes. This is the community that never tried to be virtual; it was content to live in the middle of its world and love God. There was only one name that really mattered. You can still Google it on the Web: Jesus!

It's a good place to start. It's where the church was before there was electricity, during the first two thousand years of church history. It's a set of one-on-one relationships that began in a group of fishermen who decided, according to their primitive, nonvirtual metaphor, that they ought to be fishing for men, not status and reputation. Back when a mouse was just a rodent, there was bread and wine and human need. Are these still the basic stuff of community? I think so. But it may take a while to see how it all plays out.

PART 5

Preaching Smart in a Dumb-Down Culture

We are living in a revolutionary era. Philosophically, technologically, politically, ethically and religiously, our world is in the throes of change. That well-known line from Marc Connelly's *Green Pastures* grows more and more relevant, "Everything nailed down is coming loose." It is imperative, then, that as evangelicals we engage in some hard thinking about our social responsibility. Are we faithfully obeying God's will as it has been disclosed in God's Word? Are we communicating and implementing a full-orbed Gospel? Is our version of Christianity truncated, perhaps emasculated, and therefore something far less than the dynamic it ought to be? Are we reading the Bible through the dark glasses of tradition, failing to see what it actually teaches and how it actually bears upon every dimension of life?

Vernon Grounds[1]

127

9. DEFINING OURSELVES

My entire life has been one long search for faith. I haven't found it! I do not believe in God. Having said that, . . . I want you to know that I love the idea of God. I love piety. Without it you leave your life unmoored, in a state of isolation. You are a tiny speck in a vast universe.

I'm jealous, frankly. I feel as though I have missed out on the greatest thing that can happen to a person—faith in God. It must be wonderful.

Richard Selzer[2]

10. A PLEA FOR THE MARRIAGE OF MIND AND HEART

Millions of committed Christ followers, looking for more of God, have stopped attending church on Sunday mornings. Why are they leaving? Where are they going? And what does this mean for the future of the church?

George Barna[3]

9

Defining Ourselves

About a year ago, after some concerted attention regarding my own controlling tendencies, I sensed that a significant, tectonic shift had taken place in the depth of my heart. What did it feel like? A deep joy, and awareness of more freedom in my soul, a greater range of sources than I'd had before.

Klaus Issler[1]

For years I kept the words of Nels F. S. Ferré front and center on my desk and in my mind. He wrote in 1948, "Fundamentalism, as the defender of supernaturalism, has . . . a genuine heritage, and a profound truth to preserve. . . . We shall someday thank our fundamentalist friends for having held the main fortress while countless leaders went over to the foe of a limited scientism and a shallow naturalism."[2] This was written more than sixty years ago, but if fundamentalism was strong then, it is anemic now. In fact it has lost its ability to counsel anyone on academic survival. Nels F. S. Ferré guessed at its future strength, and he guessed wrong.

> I have concluded that by the year 2025, the spiritual profile of the nation will be dramatically different. Specifically I suspect that only about one-third of the population will rely upon a local congregation as their primary or exclusive means for experiencing and expressing their faith.
>
> George Barna[3]

Across the gamut from that sixty-year-old erroneous prophecy, George Barna says the current loss of evangelical dynamism will continue to dwindle to a serious extent in the next fifteen years. Considering how far it has dwindled in the last fifteen, our prospects for reviving evangelicalism appear to be bleak indeed. Not even the once-fiery fundamentalists can turn it around. They still talk the fundamentals of the faith, but they find it increasingly hard to trump up a rally strong enough to make the Ferré prophecy even a remote possibility. Barna has plenty of statistics to rebut his dismal prophecy.

Shifting from Literacy to the Arts

The best book on the subject of the dumbing down of evangelicalism in my opinion is Mark Noll's *Scandal of the Evangelical Mind*. The book is rich with insights, but a couple of the most valuable ones reside in both a chapter title and the book's opening line. Chapter 5 of his book is called "The Intellectual Disaster of Fundamentalism." The title is enough to tell you that he also disagrees with Nels F. S. Ferré. Remember that evangelicalism is but the thinking, reading cousin of fundamentalism. The inference of this title is that fundamentalism not only is dumbing down but also is close to dumbing out. Hardly anyone confesses to being a fundamentalist any longer. George Barna believes that by 2025, one-third of those who continue to be believers will "realize their faith through the media, the arts, and other cultural institutions."[4]

There is a great deal of support being given to Barna's ideas that many evangelicals are going to be telling the traditional church to take a hike while they seek God and understanding through the arts. Given what we have said in earlier chapters about dumbing down of culture, it is reasonable that evangelicals are going to find the evangelical church too shallow in their understanding. Thus the churches will be unable to offer what these believers need to stabilize them in a culture that has become increasingly complex. Not only will it be unrelated to the avant-garde values of the culture where we are, but also of the one that is even now beginning to form.

Evangelicalism Dumbing Down, Then Out

But let us look at the opening line of Noll's book. "The scandal of the evangelical mind is that there isn't much of an evangelical mind."[5] It isn't just that the evangelical mind is dumbing down; it is also the horrible speed at which it is doing so. The dumb-down has all but destroyed most of the thinking clergy and much of the studied laity.

The loss of the evangelical mind has been obvious for years. In 1963 Harry Blamires wrote in *The Christian Mind*, "There is no longer a Christian mind. . . . The Christian mind has succumbed to the secular drift with a degree of weakness . . . unmatched in Christian history."[6] Charles Malik, in dedicating the Billy Graham Center at Wheaton in 1980, said, "I must be frank with you: the greatest danger besetting American evangelical Christianity is the danger of anti-intellectualism. The mind at its greatest and deepest reaches is not cared for enough."[7] Jonathan Edwards was a hero of the Great Awakening, but for all his love for God, he never suggested that Christians of his or any other day should close their

[Jonathan] Edwards was eager to discover what others were learning about nature, whether physical or human. He thrilled, for example, to read the works of John Locke and Sir Isaac Newton for what those works told him about human nature and the physical world.

Mark Noll[8]

eyes to books and truth. The greatest of truth was always to be found in Christ, but never did he consider secular truth to be unimportant or trivial, and he certainly never advocated that it be ignored.

Ignoring Edwards's example, the current, rapid slipping of evangelicals into the dumb-down morass is noted in this fact:

> Those more educated now tend to be significantly less religious; those more religious tend to be significantly less educated. For example, evangelicals are the only religious group in America that exceeds the national average of those not completing the eighth grade or high school. At the same time only 24 percent of evangelicals achieve some university training, compared with 68 percent of non-Christians.[9]

Evangelicals are dumbing down at twice the rate of non-Christians. That ultimately means your chances of meeting an educated American are twice as likely on the sidewalks of a city as they are inside the evangelical churches of that same city.

Dealing with the Fatal Flaws of Anti-Intellectualism

There has always been a tendency to play down the intellectual and artistic values among evangelicals. Those who work in evangelical seminaries have endured decades of hearing their graduate institutions referred to as *cemeteries*. People have been heard to slur biblical scholars as scholars who teach "Hebrew, *She-brew*, and *Home-brew*." Even scholars themselves will often demean their own intellectualism just to relate to laypeople—apparently to appear more humble by trying to look more ignorant. I heard one such intellectual say, "I got my PhD, which is like the curl in a pig's tail, a little more curlicue at the end of the pig but no more bacon in his makeup." In addition to this, one often hears preachers opt for a more dumb-down relationship by saying, "If God said it, I believe it."

I am fond of the story of a country preacher who was reading the story of Adam and Eve out of Genesis, and when he turned a page in his reading, he accidentally turned two pages. Without intending to, he landed in the flood story, so that his reading went something like this: "And Adam took Eve for his wife . . . and she was 300 cubits long and 50 cubits wide and daubed all over with slime and pitch." He suddenly realized something was amiss and stopped, and after thinking it all over, he cried out over the heads of his parishioners, "Well, praise the Lord! If God said it, I believe it." Well, of course God didn't say it, but it was his automatic way to dumb-down his mystique. The result was to dumb-down his congregation.

The Anti-Art Evangelical

Where the arts are concerned, evangelicals have been equally prone to dumb-down the artists to put more camaraderie into their sermons. This bad attitude toward art and the artists stems from a long-standing argument that began with the Reformation, when scholars in general and Calvinists in particular reacted against icons (church statuary and paintings). Their original objection to art had to do with a protest of iconic idolatry, but in recent years it has related to feelings that art is antithetical to good doctrine or religious meaning. For example, take evangelicals' reaction to the Harry Potter novels as demonic. These evangelical censors tried to discourage Christians from reading the novels on the basis that they were of the devil.

Protestant Christianity has often been maligned as being entirely anti-art, but such an idea is patently false. As for the Puritans, for instance, they actually used poetry and the arts frequently and cultivated their respect for and indulgence in the arts.

Milton, himself a Puritan, said: "If we think to regulate printing, thereby to rectify manners, we must regulate all recessions and pastimes, all that is delightful to man. No music shall be heard, no song be set or sung, but what is grave and Doric."[10] That is to say, if we start to censor the arts, we will end up with a social order that is bland and noncreative.

The heart of this kind of protest must be laid at the radical end of Calvinism. On January 1, 1519, Huldrych Zwingli (1484–1531) became the pastor of the Grossmünster Cathedral in Zurich. Soon thereafter he began preaching on reforming the Catholic church, including attacking the use of images in places of worship. Unfortunately, what the Reformers like Zwingli didn't seem to understand is that people draw and sculpt the heroes of the faith because they mean so much. Art is not prior, it is secondary. We don't paint a hero and look around for someone to admire who matches the painting. We pick the heroes and then start carving and painting.

The odd thing is that if you visit Grossmünster today, out in front of the cathedral is a statue of Zwingli. Why? Because enough people admired Zwingli to have his statue made. We can't get away from the notion that people will paint and sculpt their heroes. It doesn't do any good to criticize the idea; it is just true.

I used to tell my students that the arts and the Bible are both on the same side, and in a way they are about the same things: they are both about life; they are both about worldviews. Consider Harriet Beecher-Stowe's *Uncle Tom's Cabin*. It wasn't just a story meant to distract us; it painted a picture of the horrors of slavery. *Don Quixote* wasn't just a novel; it was a call to see the ideal, to honor the world not as it was but as it should be. No significant novel or poem is ever just that; they are a summons to the world to examine and perhaps adopt a better worldview. Perhaps the unnecessary divisions between Christ and the arts could be eliminated if we just faced the fact that all people, Christians notwithstanding, may speak in words, but all of us store our ideas in images. Our minds are not essentially ledgers full of things to be spoken or read. Our minds are essentially picture books.

> Art tries literally to picture things which philosophy tries to put into carefully thought-out words.
> Hans Rookmaaker[11]

How happy the world would be if preachers simply accepted this and began preaching in stories and images. Sermons would certainly seem shorter and would be far more memorable than mere dialectic spewed out over a drowsy world that was never quite able to fit so many dull words into the picture books of their minds.

But let us move on to ask specifically how we are to arrest the dumb-down tendencies that afflict evangelicalism, and to see if there are any reasonable ways to recover for artists and scholars the esteem they ought to have as cultural heroes.

Let me provide an example of the rejection of a great young artist who found no real place for his art in the evangelical church. A few years ago I was the guest preacher at a rather large church in Tennessee. The church's only form of worship was a contemporary service, based to-tally on guitars and percussion—no piano was used in the services at all. It struck me as very odd, since in this part of Dixie only a few years ago, guitars

> In art a worldview is made tangible.
> David Gobel[12]

and trap-sets would have been frowned on and choirs and pianos expected. But now, many pastors and church leaders want to ap-pear as far from traditional worship as possible. So it was with this particular church.

I noticed a young man playing the drums with some vigor. He was clean-cut and very handsome, and as trap players go, he also seemed very good at the percussive arts. I thought no more of it.

Following the service, the pastor invited me to his home for lunch. I hadn't been in his home long when I was surprised as the drummer boy I had noticed in the service also came in. I met him and discovered he was the pastor's son. I told him I heard him playing the drums in the services and complimented him on his talent.

> Biblical truth is so rich and multidimensional that it can affirm what is true in every worldview, while at the same time critiquing its errors and transcending its limitations. In this way, Christianity makes possible the greatest intellectual and artistic freedom.
>
> Nancy Pearcey[13]

"Well," he said, "I would rather be playing the piano, but we don't use one in the church."

This stunned me. "So there is not a way for you to use your keyboard talent in the church?"

"No, not much," he said looking down.

"Are you pretty good at the piano?"

"Well, I wouldn't say so, but I did win the Rachmaninov competition in the South last year."

"Really," I said. "Do you know his *Rhapsody on a Theme from Paganini*?" He said nothing but went over to a lovely grand piano and played my request in what seemed to me a flawless performance.

I wonder how long evangelicals will continue to discourage such great artists from finding a place of usefulness in the church. We do this in our attempt to attract our culturally trapped, rock-addicted clientele, thus thwarting all artists who do not represent our dumb-down tastes.

The church where I worship has a great soloist who only sings in the traditional service—the service where we old fuddy-duddies go to sing hymns. This is because her voice and talent do not match our worship team's style, and they are unwilling to set aside their own more contemporary taste in order to use everyone. This particular woman tells me that they have made it known to her that her style doesn't represent their outreach target.

In the case of both these gifted artists, the evangelical community forbids them the usefulness and heroism they deserve in their own local churches. At the same time, they assign hero status to lesser artists who can become popular within the contemporary context.

> Many of us have a strong allergic reaction to change of any kind. The result is an intolerance for non-conforming ideas that run like a dark streak through human history.
> William Sloan Coffin[14]

I used to think that churches who were averse to change were old-fashioned congregations who wanted to sing "The Old Rugged Cross" in a post–Jimmy Hendrix world. But I have learned that in their Lady Gaga cultural context, the contemporary church is just as averse to singing the "Diadem."[15]

Recently I preached in a church whose motto is, "Come just as you are to worship." I did, and the contemporary guards met me at the door with a pair of scissors, threatening to cut off my necktie if I didn't take it off. They obviously didn't mean, "Come just as you are"; they meant, "Come just as we want you to," especially if you are the preacher for the day. A reluctance to change is as firmly planted in the contemporary mindset as it ever was in the traditional mindset.

Conclusion

Being contemporary is for many of our age a one-dimensional mindset. The richness of our culture in all its expressions is bolted down to a single, allowable art form: the folk-rock format. It is a mindset that considers it a sin to allow neckties in the front door or choir robes in the side door. All kinds of church dress are forbidden except for the most casual styles.

Art never really develops unless it is set free to embrace its freedom to vary from the norm. The worst thing about artistic restrictions is that they don't merely develop one-dimensional congregations, they limit the attendance of all whose dimensions are varied. If it was spurring church growth, that would be one mark of approval, but it actually seems to be working against the church. We cannot help but wonder if the evangelicals who are vanishing first are those who found no place for their personal taste in worship. Lord, come and heal our prejudices. Widen our acceptance.

10

A Plea for the Marriage of Mind and Heart

> Public reverses for fundamentalism in the 1920s seemed
> to signal the end of intellectual vitality among conser-
> vative evangelicals. Before too long, however, ambi-
> tious young preachers, scholars and journalists who
> had been raised as fundamentalists frankly rejected
> the dispensationalism of their heritage. . . . Harold
> John Ockenga (1905–1985) . . . called for a *new evan-
> gelicalism* that would value scholarship and take an
> active interest in society while maintaining traditional
> Protestant orthodoxy.
>
> Mark Noll[1]

Contemporary pastor Rob Bell recently jettisoned the word *hell*
from his teaching. Shortly after he did this, many other pastors
jumped on him with academic tar and feathers to force him to
return to orthodoxy. One pastor entitled his scathing denuncia-
tion of Bell "Farewell, Rob Bell!" When N. T. Wright made known

what some considered his unwelcome deviancies on Pauline theologies, he reaped an immediate barrage of criticism from other theologians.

I do not comment on whether to condemn or bless those who appear to depart from orthodoxy on any subject. I only know that scathing the heretics makes us look cantankerous to a wide-eyed culture who can never figure out why we take our theology so seriously in the first place. Usually these denunciations come with a highly enthusiastic display of criticism. No wonder William Sloan Coffin said, "I only trust sad soldiers. I only trust sad revolutionaries. The enthusiastic ones are always out to get someone."[2]

We may not always agree with either the thinking or the declarations of scholars, but we ought to leave them to express their viewpoints, even when we think they are off track or out of sync with Christians as a whole. Does this mean that we should give scholars the right to vary from the "faith which was once for all delivered to the saints" (Jude 3 NKJV)? Is there such a faith?

Yes there is! But we are all at variance even with that definition. There are honestly good scholars who disagree about what the "faith which was once delivered to the saints" really was. Nancy Pearcey reminds us that early Christian truth was always unitive, but I don't necessarily agree with her on this. Fierce arguments have always raged within the church about the nature of truth. But in the best of their endeavors, the early church fathers wanted to provide simple, formulaic creeds to which all believers could ascribe. And thinking back on the Nicene Creed and the Apostles' Creed, they largely succeeded. We can only deduce that the scholars who formulated those creeds must have slept very well after they participated in constructing a code of agreement that was very specific

> The early church insisted that biblical truth is a comprehensive unity . . . truth is a unified whole. Today Christians have largely lost that conviction.
>
> Nancy Pearcey[3]

while still allowing Christians to pursue a wide range of biblical studies in which they did not agree totally.

That was a good day. May it be born again. May scholars believe as the Spirit working within their individuality leads them to believe. This happy day would end the fierce disagreements between Calvinists and Arminians. This could breed free scholarship that would bless the church because of its freedom and variety. Personally, I have never liked hunting down heretics. I discovered that when I find heretics and identify them, they are not as evil as they are earnest. And I prefer to work on the wide creeds that help me identify my friends rather than on the narrower ones designed to help me locate my enemies. I believe it is true that the Spirit bears witness that we are the children of God, and I don't feel comfortable going against the Spirit—the great identifier of the kingdom's children—just so I can enjoy feeling doctrinally superior to others. Most of the time what we quibble over is not significant.

> Switching from a Methodist church to a Presbyterian church is not transformational.
> George Barna[4]

I served on the translation committee of the Christian Standard Bible. It was an honor, and I am grateful for the privilege. Even though it was a Southern Baptist effort, I found myself meeting a lot of Presbyterian translators. I was amazed that I liked them so much. It's true that they don't baptize adults, and they have always put a little more content into infant baptisms than I wish they would. And individually they could be a bit strong-headed about predestination and elder governance. But they were so darn nice! And then the Holy Spirit started bearing witness that we are all the children of God. Everywhere I turned I ran into the Apostles' Creed. So I formulated a mass acceptance of Presbyterian scholars. The evangelical church does not need to be afraid to welcome scholars into their midst and then set them free to be who they are: Christians with a love of truth.

Encouraging the Marriage of Passion and Study

Unfortunately, dumbing down in time usually adds up to *dumbing out*. To lose contact with either scholars or thinkers will in time further marginalize evangelicals. To halt this mad rush to irrelevancy, I call for a balance between passion and study.

The broad theological categories for these values are two words: *kerygma* and *didache*. The word *kerygma* refers to the more passionate, feeling side of the gospel. And the word *didache* refers to the more intellectually demanding, study side of the gospel. When *kerygma* is missing, we refer to Christianity as dull, boring, and insipid. When *didache* is missing, we refer to church as lite, adolescent, giddy, and irrelevant. *Kerygma only* is the church without a brain. *Didache only* is the church without a heart.

> Millions of devout followers of Jesus Christ are repudiating tepid systems and practices of the Christian faith and introducing a wholesale shift in how faith is understood, integrated, and influencing the world.
>
> George Barna[5]

George Barna makes it clear that the evolution of the church of the future is going to demand this integration for all who choose to follow Christ. If there is to be a church, it will be a church that marries the heart and mind. He says:

> There are four macro-models of church experience resident in the nation today. The dominant force is the congregational form of the church. House churches—some call them simple church fellowships—are yet another holistic model. These small congregations . . . meet in someone's home on a regular basis to fulfill all the functions of a traditional congregation, especially elements such as worship, teaching, fellowship and stewardship. . . .
>
> The family faith is a third holistic model in which the family becomes the primary spiritual unit and pursues faith matters together, with parents and their children (and often members of the extended family) becoming a close-knit faith community. The fourth

holistic model is cyberchurch. This refers to the range of spiritual experiences delivered through the internet.[6]

Why this headlong rush away from the congregational form? The members of the house church have found larger churches lacking in passion or depth or both.

Either wittingly or not, Calvinist evangelicals have brought a sense of content to Christianity. But they have always been dubbed more cerebral than warm (hence the term *frozen chosen*). They have not usually made significant contributions to the emotional side of the equation. Much of the megachurch movement has built excitement into the mix—and excitement is just one more facet of *kerygma*, or passion—but they have often been dubbed as *church lite*. Either one of these movements will be inadequate for the church of 2025.

C. S. Lewis will long be regarded as the dominant scholar in the twentieth century because he managed to find a way to be holistic regarding these values. His stories and theological books warmed evangelicals with his passion. His conversion became a real point of identity with all evangelicals. Even Baptists and Pentecostals read his works and felt a real identity with how similar the story of his conversion was to their own. His passion about it was similar to those who led evangelical thinking in America in particular.

Lewis's conversion solved for him the difficulty of keeping his feelings for Jesus in one pocket and his need for logic in the other. As Nancy Pearcey puts it:

> Christ's life, death and resurrection were events that occurred in the physical world, testable by the same means as any other historical event. Yet they were also the fulfillment of the ancient myths that Lewis had always loved. He used the term *myth* not to mean a story that is false but one that answers the deep human longing for transcendence.[7]

143

The reason that evangelicals so love Lewis and so distrust themselves is that they have not put the solid bottom of reason on their leaky, feeling-saturated souls. Sound the organ, let the wedding of mind and heart begin! We must accomplish this marriage or perish. In the last decade and a half we have already lost between 12 and 15 percent of our attendance.

We cannot long keep any vitality about us at this rate of decline. We must do better than this in the years to come for two reasons. First, if we do not, we will find ourselves on a fast-paced march to cultural irrelevancy. Second, we ourselves will be increasingly forced to admit that our absentee discipleship has stolen our desire to inform our faith. As the title of this book indicates, evangelicals will vanish, as T. S. Eliot said, "Not with a bang but a whimper."

Returning the Parson to Be the Person of the Parish

For the church to manage the new unity of mind and heart, there is one imperative: the wedding of passion and truth. The key minister to officiate at such a marriage is the local church pastor. Traditionally the word *parson* derived from the notion that the parson was the *person of the parish*. In a small English or American village, the parson was the best educated and the most thoroughly acquainted with Scripture, so he became the wise man of the town, full of wisdom and good judgment. Consider this corollary truth: Theodore Roszak says that the best role model for a parson is the shaman. Why? Because in primitive villages the tribal people see the shaman as a mysterious soul through whom strange forces pass.[8]

In Jane Austen's *Pride and Prejudice*, the Reverend Mr. Collins is summoned into the library at Longbourn because Mary Bennet (who, by the way, has been reading Fordyce's sermons) has a problem of great doctrinal import. Who better to help her figure things out than the Reverend Mr. Collins?

In those days pastors were seen as counselors and representatives of God. The world was somewhat like that in the middle of the twentieth century, when I assumed my first parish. I was a young pastor with all of the liabilities of ignorance that goes with too much esteem too early in my uninformed life. People always seemed to want to talk to me about all kinds of matters, especially those that related to the church. I did the best I could, but I was totally inadequate to serve them well. It is strange, however, that when a pastor comes into the counseling room robed in an intention of serving a holy God, the Holy Spirit himself sees to it that all that is said comes wrapped in the garb of divine mystery.

I did come to understand two things: First, there was a kind of trust that went with my office. It humbled me, and I determined to be a *world Christian* as fast as I could. This impression guided me for my next thirty-five years of pastoral ministry. I had always been a reader, and a reader of

> The Christian faith has only one object: the mystery of Christ dead and risen. . . . It is accomplished historically in the earthly life of Christ, it is contained in mystery in the sacraments, it is lived mystically in souls, it is accomplished socially in the Church, it is consummated eschatologically in the heavenly kingdom.
>
> Jean Danielou[9]

the best books, but the way they trusted me inspired me to better understand the arts and current events. If I was going to help them become world Christians, I felt I should be the best one I could. But becoming a world Christian isn't just examining the arts; it is living and encountering them. Life isn't where we live, it is our teacher, and it both gives to us and adds to our worldview. We are assembling the ledger of our counsel out of all we have touched.

Second, I learned why Catholics call their clerics *Father*. It was this paternalistic feeling that led me to become engaged to my pilgrimage. Even the men—especially the men—came to me for prayer and counsel. It amazed me that men twice my age listened to my advice as though I was competent to advise them. They seemed to listen like a child listens to a parent. This humbled me, and it made me seek God for answers to help them walk through their days.

So in bringing about the marriage of knowledge and passion, the passion derives from the pastor's walk with God, and he will never be any better at disseminating passion than he is in using it as his own pathway to intimacy with the great mystery that comes in knowing Christ. Staying in touch with the mystery is the most important part of the marriage; without that there is no power. But being informed is the place where pastors are often lacking.

> All spiritual legacy work starts with reflection. You must think about your life, not just exist in it. You must, at least occasionally, chew on it, walk around it, poke at it, analyze it, make assessments of it.
>
> Daniel Taylor[10]

I have no recent statistics on this, but not so long ago the average Baptist pastor read only three books a year. They were also not schooled in their appreciation of the arts and seldom attended artistic presentations.

If art is the mirror held up to philosophy and philosophy is the distillation of a worldview, then art becomes the best instructor of philosophers and artists because they help others see and interpret their world. Does a preacher need to study Degas or Warhol? How else can he hold his own Christ-centered worldview against the secular views by which the world increasingly is nourished and exhibit to his congregation the clear difference between the two?

The Pastor: The *Holder-Upper* of the Cultural Mirror

In evangelism and missions, what we are really doing is holding our worldview up to potential converts and asking them to make a decision about finding the best light for the pathway of their earthly sojourn. In her wonderful study of art and worldview, Nancy Pearcey says, "There are many good books that discuss Christian aesthetics or a biblical justification for the arts. . . . The question I am asking is not whether these works are beautiful or well executed, but how they give a pictorial expression to a worldview."[11] Pastors should know all they can about the world from which they want to lead people as well as the world they want to lead people to. We must become world Christians in order to help all those we can to change worlds.

Remember, though, that it is not adding what the Bible is to our understanding of the arts. The Bible itself is the finest example of the arts. It is full of literature, allusions, and symbols. It is the story of a great people and their search for meaning in their trek through monotheism toward messianism. I am always amused when I hear papers being read on "Art and the Scriptures" as though the Scriptures aren't art. How foolish the assumption.

> Israel in ancient days, not only had a view of Sinai in a blaze, but learned the gospel too: The types and figures were a glass in which they saw a Savior's face.
> William Cowper (1711–1800)

Surely, knowing this, our view of God ought to be enlarged, and so should our desire to be world Christians.

Conclusion

It goes without saying that preachers need an education. Whether formal or informal is not the point. The point is that without a lust to know all we can about the world and to create our own worldview, how can we ever really understand the rigors of our calling? All of us would rather hear a preacher who knows a great deal and tells us only a little than a preacher who tells us all he knows. This is because the first preacher is so rich with substance that he doesn't have time in a sermon to speak very much of what he knows. On the other hand, the second preacher tells us everything he knows in a very long sermon, but he goes on with an empty oratory that furnishes us nothing.

If heaven is the presence of all important truths, then hell must be the absence of all significance. Hell is a place for lonely, empty minds. T. S. Eliot describes it well in *The Cocktail Party*. This writer draws from his reserve the power of his own worldview, which it would do us all well to know, and describes hell as oneself, alone, "always alone."[12] Could the apostles have described any better the center of our evangelism than this poet and playwright? I think not. Nor could anything better serve our worldview than what exists in Eliot's.

Learn the world, not to emulate it but to define it, both as it is and as it will be once the renovation of the planet is complete.

A very literary fisherman wrote long ago:

> Then I saw "a new heaven and a new earth," for the first heaven and the first earth had passed away, and there was no longer any sea. I saw the Holy City, the new Jerusalem, coming down out of heaven from God, prepared as a bride beautifully dressed for her husband. And I heard a loud voice from the throne saying, "Look! God's dwelling place is now among the people, and he will dwell with them. They will be his people, and God himself will be with them and be their God. 'He will wipe every tear from their eyes. There will be no more death' or mourning or crying or pain, for the old order of things has passed away."
>
> He who was seated on the throne said, "I am making everything new!"

> Revelation 21:1–5

PART 6

The Secular Onslaught

In 1959 C. P. Snow published a book called *The Two Cultures*, warning that Western culture has split in two. In his words, a "gulf of mutual incomprehension" and "hostility" divides the sciences (chemists, engineers, physicists, and biologists) from the humanities (poets, painters, novelists, and philosophers—whom he called "literary intellectuals") . . . we have seen how right he was.

Since Snow wrote those words, the gulf has widened into a grand canyon. . . . Science and technology have continued their march forward, confident that all problems can be solved by scientific methodology. By contrast, artists and writers no longer believe that they have any significant truth to offer.

Nancy Pearcey[1]

11. LIONS TEN, CHRISTIANS ZERO

England offers a model example of de-Christianization. Of
a population of around 60 million, the number adhering to
non-Christian religions is still not large. Jews, Muslims, Sikhs
and Hindus combined represent no more than 5 percent of
the British total, roughly the same non-Christian proportion
as in the United States. But we cannot safely conclude that
the remaining 95 percent of British people should be clas-
sified as Christian. According to a survey taken in 2000,
44 percent of the British claim no religious affiliation whatever, a number that has grown from 31 percent in 1983.

Philip Jenkins[2]

12. THE CULTURE OF SECULAR CITIES

The body of Christ is at a crossroads right now. The two
common alternatives are to move either to the left or to
the right. It's our observation, however, that we are living
in a unique time, when people are frozen as they look in
either of those two directions. When they look to the left
they decide they cannot venture there. When they look to
the right they feel the same.

Whether they realize it or not, people are looking for
a fresh alternative—a third way. The crossroads today, we
believe, is one of moving forward or backward.

Leonard Sweet and Frank Viola[3]

11

Lions Ten, Christians Zero

> American society is marked by a central stress upon
> personal achievement, especially secular occupational
> achievement. The "success story" and the respect it
> accorded to the self-made man are distinctly American
> if anything is.
>
> Robin Williams[1]

In George Bernard Shaw's play *Androcles and the Lion*, a great
crowd of Christians have been rounded up to be martyred in Rome.
They are surrounded by a crowd of legionaries who force them
to keep up their pace, and they are remarkably compliant as they
march along the Via Appia to their death. To while away the dull
hours in transit to the arena, they begin singing, "Feed us to the
lions, we shall be devoured," to the tune of "Onward Christian Soldiers, Marching as to War." The melody is brisk and their anthem is
enthusiastic, and the guards are a bit annoyed by their cheerfulness.

I don't know all that Shaw was trying to say (and he was a bit of a cynic), but one thing he seemed to be saying was that Christians have always been captive to the world in which they live. Probably they have never been more captive to the secular culture than they are now. Hauerwas and Willimon in their 1989 bestseller, *Resident Aliens*, point out rather point-blank that even twenty years ago, Christians were waking up and saying, this is no longer our world.[3] Since the birth of our republic, all of us would have to confess, evangelicals increasingly have felt that America is not a Christian country anymore.

> The truth is that even if we are not captive to our culture, we look like we are. Nietzsche must have thought so too, for he said, "Christians should look more redeemed."
>
> William Sloane Coffin[2]

Supreme Court Justice David Brewer (1837–1910) said that America was "of all the nations of the world . . . most justly called a Christian nation." He said this because "Christianity has so largely shaped and molded it." Barack Obama said during his visit to Turkey in 2009, "We do not consider ourselves a Christian nation or a Jewish nation or a Muslim nation. We consider ourselves a nation of citizens who are bound by ideals and a set of values."[4]

Robert Bork wrote, "We have redefined what we mean by such things as child abuse, rape, and racial or sexual discrimination so that behavior until recently thought quite normal, unremarkable, even benign, is now identified as blameworthy or even criminal. Middle-class life is portrayed as oppressive and shot through with pathologies. 'As part of the vast social project of moral leveling,' Krauthammer wrote, 'it is not enough for the deviant to be normalized. The normal must be found to be deviant.'"[5]

In other words, good values must be made to look boring and passé. Christians have come to look upon their deviancy as experimental and even normal or fun. Hence we have become indistinguishable from the culture we once thought needed to be redeemed.

We are now—as most secular philosophers like to think of it—a secular state. But how did we get here from where we were, and even more important, when did the nation become secular? Charles Krauthammer[6] says the culture became normal in their own eyes as people redefined deviancy. What then happened to our self-esteem, and what caused the change in the way we view ourselves? The change of culture is shown in Will Willimon's story of how the youth in the Methodist Youth Fellowship of Greenville, South Carolina, came across a distinct demarcation of the age.

Sometime between 1960 and 1980, an old, inadequately conceived world ended and a fresh new world began . . . sometime on a Sunday evening in 1963. Then in Greenville, South Carolina, in defiance of the state's time-honored blue laws, the Fox Theater opened on Sunday. Seven of us—regular attenders of the Methodist Youth Fellowship at Buncombe Street Church—made a pact to enter the front door of the church, be seen, then quietly slip out the back door and join John Wayne at the Fox. That evening came to represent a watershed in the history of Christendom, South Carolina style. On that night, Greenville, South Carolina—the last pocket of resistance to secularity in the Western world—served notice that it would no longer be a prop for the church. There would be no more free passes for the church, no more free rides. The Fox Theater went head to head with the church over who would provide the worldview for the young. That night in 1963, the Fox Theater won the opening skirmish.[8]

> Senior devil Screwtape to junior devil Wormwood:
>
> Prosperity knits a man to the World. He feels he is "finding his place in it," while really it is finding its place in him. His increasing reputation, his widening circle of acquaintances, his sense of importance, the growing pressure of absorbing and agreeable work, build up in him a sense of being really at home on Earth, which is just what we want.
>
> C. S. Lewis[7]

But the Methodist youth may already have been staring in the face of American prosperity, which in a score of years began eroding all churches, the Methodists too. Prosperity is the brother of secularism. Jesus said it is hard to serve God and money (Matt. 6:24), and money is the foundation of our capitalist, secular world. Prosperity requires the pursuit of the whole person. It is an avid appetite, which in time can turn martyrs into plutocrats.

In a million such skirmishes in villages and great cities all across America, from Hollywood to Times Square, the secular age has triumphed over the Christian world. And like the martyrs in Shaw's play, the lions won, the Christians lost. I've always wondered if those mauled by the beasts looked up to the hordes in the stands and wondered what it must be like to see the death of Christians—to have secularians watch the death of the religious. But in the fullness of time, we are being permitted to watch the death of evangelicalism while we crowd out the apathetic arenas of our own world.

> Since American culture is a variant of all Western democracies, this may really be a book about Western decline. In the United States, at least, that decline and the mounting resistance to it have produced what we now call a culture war. It is impossible to say what the outcome will be, but for the moment our trajectory continues downward.[9]

> David Lyon cites consumerism and new information technologies as the reason for this cultural shift. Our consumeristic attitude toward religion is a natural outgrowth of capitalism. What if we stopped marketing Christianity? Would it be more authentic? Would we be?
> Dave Tomlinson[10]

Not to quibble over semantics, it may be more honest for us to say we are in a *subculture* war since evangelicals are a resistant culture to secular life. This term may be more honest because we are so much owned by the secular culture that we cannot claim to be separated from it. Indeed, for the past several decades, we have been in the midst of a cultural shift into the middle of secularism. Our values have so eroded that we have smuggled lasers into our secular comfort zone.

It was William Wordsworth who spoke to me about the easy danger of materialism, which is the porch of secularism.

> The world is too much with us: late and soon,
> Getting and spending, we lay waste our powers.[11]

Secularism means *this-world-ism*, and it is the ever-encroaching philosophy at the gates of every generation of Christian history.

Dealing with Three Secular Syncretisms

Wordsworth objected to the emotional high cost of getting-and-spending materialism, which may be the biggest contributor to our addiction to secularism. But it is not the only one. There are two other ways that secularism has wormed its way into our inability to stop the erosion of evangelicalism.

1. Christian Materialism

In late December of 2011, new Air Jordan athletic shoes came into our country from a foreign manufacturer and hit the store shelves during the last week before Christmas. This initiated a wave of crash shopping when hordes of shoppers broke through police and riot lines and actually broke through the glass of shop windows to be one of the lucky ones who actually got to purchase a two-hundred-dollar pair of sneakers. This phenomenon is but an example of the rampant nature of American materialism. But it isn't just America that has been bitten by secular material-ism. It's the whole world.

> In 1977, Deng Xiaoping put China on the road to capitalism declaring, "to get rich is glorious."
> Thomas Friedman[12]

In America's secular, materialistic Christmas events, Black Fri-day most clearly points out our insane addiction to materialism. After getting up at two or three in the morning (some stores now stay open the entire night) and shopping in packed malls, there are tales of fistfights and of spraying competing customers with mace and pepper spray to get to the first place in cash-register lines. In a world where two-thirds of the population goes to bed hungry every night, our American consumerism must spark a wave of nausea around the globe.

In the economic downturn that has plagued our country since 2008, there have been several stimulus injections to fuel a new wave of consumer spending. The amount of the funds reached upwards of a trillion dollars. During that same time the issuance of food stamps moved from over twenty million stamps to over forty million. The lower 20 percent of those living in poverty were still bombarded with newspaper and television ads crying for them to spend even more money in a year of flatline economic growth.

The downturn of the US economy since 2008 still has not calmed our ardent material pursuits. We still care fervently about getting on in the world. The countless books that talk about how to get wealthy and how to stay wealthy continue to be produced at a breakneck speed. The old question that Malcolm Boyd asked in the previous generation is still the most-asked question among

An American auto parts manufacturer in China posted the following African proverb, translated into Mandarin, on his factory floor:

> Every morning in Africa, a gazelle wakes up.
> It knows it must run faster than the fastest lion
>   or it will be killed.
> Every morning a lion wakes up.
> It knows it must outrun the slowest gazelle
>   or it will starve to death.
> It doesn't matter whether you are
>   a lion or a gazelle.
> When the sun comes up, you better start running.[13]

156

all driven executives and is still the one driving the schedules of Christian entrepreneurs. His question (and consequently his book title) is, "Are you running with me, Jesus?"[14]

If the motto of materialism is, "Everyone is chasing the almighty buck," then the motto of Christian secularism must be, "Everyone is chasing their best standing in a world where Christ is not their most cherished loyalty." They are simply trying to get on in the world that is at hand—and hang those who are in the way.

2. The Invasion of the Open Secular Syncretism

Whenever Christianity bumps into others cultures, it changes the culture it interfaces with and consequently is changed by that culture. When Christians bumped into the Roman festival Saturnalia, a winter festival was born that we now call Christmas. When it bumped into Celtic culture, we picked up Easter—named after Eostre, a pre-Christian goddess of fertility, whose fecund symbol may have been rabbits and eggs. This syncretism did not benefit the Christian side of the equation. We gave the Romans a Christian Saturnalia, and in time we got back Frosty and Rudolph. We traded Bethlehem for a North Pole workshop full of elves. We gave Celts the resurrection, and they gave us back bunnies, eggs, and daffodils.

But in bumping into secular culture, Christianity has experienced the most deviant of exchanges. We gave the secular culture the keys to the kingdom; they gave us back political correctness. We gave them a rich heritage of missionary martyrs, hospitals, and universities; they gave us back PowerPoint announcements, Jumbotrons, and an odd mixture of values. We cried out for them to "come to Christ alone and be saved," and they told us we could be saved in any number of ways, by any number of saviors. We said, "Seek Christ and be like us"; they said, "Seek riches and be like us." They won. Their novels and movies in just a decade or two caused our young men and women to move in together for no higher calling than merely to share the rent. They traded in their Bibles at adult bookstores.

We at first condemned their dark values in church, then they quit coming to church. So we changed the church. We emerged. We thought this would lure them back. We played their kind of music, danced their kind of dances, never again said a word about sin, and winked at their shame. We never mentioned hell, or we toned down its impact so that nobody ever went there except Adolf and Saddam. So our surrender of the doctrine wasn't much of a surrender. Yet even these accommodations didn't win them over. We still looked so much like the secularians that we were indistinguishable.

A new race is evolving: the *Christo-secularians*. Some of them still go to church, but most of them see no real point in it. We haggle daily in the marketplace over what kind of commitment creates a marriage and what defines it. We fuss over how much of trusting God should be allowed on our coins, or how many nativity sets you can put in one park, or whether the Ten Commandments be displayed in any taxpayer-supported courtroom.

Expositional Bible preaching is being squeezed out of the north and into Dixie and Texas. The division between the secularians and the Christo-secularians is all but geographical now. Most of those who still cling to the old ways now live in the southern states. North of the Mason-Dixon line, stretching between Hollywood and New York, is considered the land of the secularians. There in the forward-thinking states, the syncretism is nearing completion. The case is clear: we are becoming two completely separate cultures. It is as C. P. Snow said it would be fifty years ago. In his book *The Two Cultures,* he warned that the division of the cultures, notably in science and the arts, was on its way. But the division goes much deeper than that. There has come about a complete division in worldviews: the Christian worldview and the secular worldview.

3. Sexual Syncretism

The contemporary culture is so saturated in sexual imagery that we seem to be in a morass, and the quicksand is sucking us downward into irrelevancy. Nancy Pearcey attests in her book *Saving Leonardo* that Anne Lamott is a favorite author for young evangelicals.[15] Having heard her speak to emergent church gatherings, I know she is right. Many passages in Lamott's books could cause even Janet Evanovich to blush. They are so filled with sexual imagery that I wonder if a part of her appeal to contemporary Christians is due to the fact that her readers have lived so long in sexual concord with the culture that they have been weaned from all things holy and proper.

There is no question that contemporary Christians have lost the sense of modesty that belonged to the more Victorian generation that gave them birth. And of course they can never go back to that less frank mystique their parents possessed. After the publication of *Operating Instructions* in 1993, Lamott's critics praised her for being "honest" (*San Francisco Examiner*), "glib and gritty" (the *Kirkus Reviews*), "irreverent" (the *Library Journal*), and "candid" (*Publishers Weekly*). If contemporary Christians were fans when the book was published in 1993, they must really exalt her now. I only cite her popularity with Christians to demonstrate that Bork was right. We are not just Jesus followers in our day, we are the sexually soaked Jesus followers who are too immersed in the sexual culture to have anything left to say to it.

There are also gentle and acceptable signs that we are growing closer to the avant-garde sexual side of the culture. In something as gentle as online dating services, ChristianMingle.com looks a lot like Match.com minus some amoral features frightened off by the word *Christian*. In other words, it's probably just an adjective away from the indulgent business of computer matchup—thank God for the adjective! Having lost the struggle to keep Easter bunnies out of Christianity, in our own millennium we are losing the struggle to keep Hugh Hefner's bunnies from lobbying for Christian acceptance.

When I first began to follow Jerry Falwell's ministry, I thought of him as somewhat of a brother. He founded the Thomas Road Baptist Church in 1956, only ten years before I began planting the Westside Baptist Church in Omaha. Following in his queue of influence emerged the Moral Majority movement. Most of the time I found that his moral crusades did indeed belong to the majority, but sometimes it seemed he and his organization trivialized the great moral issues of the day that were already beginning to show some compromise with the secular invasion of the times. There was the instance of his protest of a Virginia bakery that baked gingerbread men complete with genitals. Gingerbread nudies seemed a minor place to begin a righteous crusade to restore or even affirm the Moral Majority. Then in the late nineties there was the accusation that the Teletubbies character Tinky Winky was gay—on exactly what basis I can't recall. Once again it seemed a weak protest of the sweeping revision of American morals that could have been attacked. But apart from sexually explicit gingerbread men and gay Teletubbies, I think most American evangelicals were on his side.

The real problem was that even at that time, the flagrant cultural attack of the most immoral sort was rising: the new rock-rap music by which the culture was establishing open sexuality that almost no one addressed. As Robert Bork remarks in his remarkable book *Slouching towards Gomorrah*:

> The obscenity of thought and word is staggering. . . . The lyrics often range from the perverse to the mercifully unintelligible. It is difficult to convey just how debased rap is.[16]

The Moral Majority was unable to check the rapid deterioration of the arts and seemed to make no impact at all when the nation, led by such organizations as the National Endowment for the Arts, supported the downward trend. I became somewhat involved in the attempt to slow down the descent in a debate at Charleston Southern University. The late Chip Conyers arranged the debate between me and an official of the NEA on the college campus during the Spoleto Arts Festival. The university at that time was an institution supported by Southern Baptists, and the debate focused mainly on the homoerotic art of Robert Mapplethorpe. If there was a winner of the debate, it would have been me (after all, this was at a Baptist university, and the audience's sensibilities were aligned in my direction from the start).

This particular debate was one of many across America to protest Mapplethorpe's photos on display in a prominent gallery. At the same time, Andre Serrano's "Piss Christ" (a crucifix immersed in a beaker of urine) created national controversy due to government funding.[17] These pictures were graphically phallic, and the question was whether the National Endowment for the Arts should be allowed to finance a showing of that sort with taxpayer money. It was an easy argument to win in the South.

Concerning the issue of whether tax money should support such exhibits, I took Robert Bork's position long before his book was published:

> We seem too timid to state that Mapplethorpe's and Serrano's pictures should not be shown in public, whoever pays for them. We are going to have to overcome that timidity if our culture is not going to decline still further.[18]

While this is the crux of Bork's fifteen-year-old warning, it is even more true of us today.

Conclusion

The Judeo-Christian world must insist on the endurance of our values. If our way of life is to remain on the earth, there must be a renaissance of biblical values, and a re-education of Christian youth that will stabilize the covenant faith of their parents. This is not a renaissance that can muddle through, slowing the preservation of our way of life. The day is late. The time to begin is now.

12

The Culture of Secular Cities

What we want, if men become Christians at all, is to keep them in a state of mind I call "Christianity And." You know—Christianity and the Crisis, Christianity and the New Psychology, Christianity and the New Order, Christianity and Faith Healing, Christianity and Psychical Research, Christianity and Vegetarianism, Christianity and Spelling Reform. If they must be Christians, let them at least be Christians with a difference. Substitute for the faith itself some Fashion with a Christian coloring. Work on their horror of the Same Old Thing.

senior devil Screwtape to junior devil Wormwood
in C. S. Lewis's *Screwtape Letters*[1]

I once believed that evangelicals intentionally adopt secular ideas and programs to intentionally try to appeal to the secularians. But the longer I observe the evangelical carbon paper, the more I have come to believe that we do not adopt secular ideas in every case to win the secular but because we are all such secular captives that we think and live as secular people while attempting to be like Jesus. I have watched evangelicals over a period of sixty years, and I can see how our increasing state of secularity has caused us to whitewash a great many secular movements and Christianize them and call ourselves *creative*.

The Myth That Must Die: To Win the Secular, Evangelicals Must Become Secular

There have been any number of these *borrow-and-sanctify* movements, but let's take the men's movement as an example. In the 1970s, the poet Robert Bly began exploring his feminine side and said that men who were emotionally healthy leaned toward his doctrine. He wrote poems and lectured on his new men's doctrine all around the United States. Then in the 1990s his new book, *Iron John*, exploded into the mass market, increasing his influence; Bly and the secular men's movement sprang to life. His thinking was that men need to get in touch with this softer side of their psyche if they are ever going to be the true men they are intended to be. It is okay for men to cry, change diapers, like ballet, wear cologne, and so on. So men who agreed with Bly began to *man down*, going to outdoor sensitivity groups, consciousness groups, and so on.

The book Bly and the guys held as their guide is the Grimm fairy tale *Iron John* (*Eisenhans* in German; *Eisen* is the word for *iron*, and *Hans* is a diminutive word for *Johann* or *John*). The tale is too complex to retell, but these are the essentials: While hunting in the woods, a hunter comes upon a dark pond, and a hand reaches up out of the water and snatches his dog (*life's circumstances happen suddenly and without warning*). The hunter then runs into town and tells the men of the village what has happened, and they all return with the hunter and dip the water out of the pond (*we are all looking for ourselves*). When all of the water has been removed, they find a huge, hairy creature at the bottom of the pond—Iron John. They lock him in a huge cage (*aren't all our alter egos locked and imprisoned within the dark waters of our inwardness?*), and the key is given to the queen, who soon gives birth to a prince (*only our mothers hold the key to our self-understanding*). Years later, as the prince nears maturity, he steals the key to the cage and releases Iron John, who in the process of counseling the prince, becomes a kind, generous, and soft man.

The story took hold, and men coast to coast began ferreting through their locked-up feminine nature looking for the aboriginal Iron John they supposed themselves to be. They all began to

> *Newsweek's* cover for June 24, 1991, displayed a grinning, bare-chested CEO holding a toddler in one arm and a conga drum in the other. Probably no one was more surprised than its author when the book Bly described as simply "an amplification of a fairy story" became a de facto Bible for what appeared to be a genuine mass movement.[2]

weep freely at their meetings while others said, "Now, now, dea-rie!" cooing in oft-motherly voices. They sometimes met in outdoor circles around bonfires, took off their shirts, played bongos, and

> Respected Christian pollster George Barna recently said that no significant movement of God really occurred among men during the last decade. In fact, he said, the condition of American men declined. "Some good things have happened among men during the 1990s," says Barna's report, *The State of the Church, 2000*, "but it does not appear that there has been massive reawakening of the male soul in the last ten years."
>
> Among America's 94 million men, only 26 million attend church, and 85 percent of all currently unchurched men were previously churchgoers, Barna says. He notes a small proportional increase in American men who claim to be "born again," but he adds that church attendance, Sunday-school attendance, and church volunteerism are down among men.
>
> Patrick Morley[3]

read poetry as enthusiastically as they once smoked cigars and watched *Monday Night Football*. It was a lot of liberation at once, but old Iron John was glad to be out of his cage at last.

So what did the movement look like when evangelical men adopted it? Well it was somewhat like the secular movement, minus the getting in touch with your feminine side. By the end of the 1990s it was just about over, and though almost a million men went to Washington, DC, for the Stand in the Gap gathering in 2011, only 13,000 attended the national meeting of Promise Keepers. Perhaps George Barna's conclusion of the lasting ineffectiveness of the Christian men's movement was that, unlike the secular movement, it was not able to appeal to all men. Sadly missing all the way along was one obviously absent group: almost the entire cadre of professional and artistic men.

Perhaps the football stadiums were the appropriate place to hold the rallies. I preached a lot across America in those days, and in virtually every church-sponsored meeting in which I preached, it was promoted with an almost threatening tone to get men to attend the rallies. I for one was so turned off by the heavy promotion it took to fill the regional stadiums that I determined to keep away from all who pushed the Promise Keeper agenda within the local church.

What Kind of Impact Did Christian Copycatting Really Have on Secular Culture?

Generally speaking, when Christians emulated the secular movements, they did it poorly. ChristianMingle.com emulates eHarmony.com. Many secular cell-group movements have been copied by Christians, emulating various sensitivity groups, but far less successfully. Actually, in many cases Christian groups have taken the names of secular movements and simply added the words *for Jesus* after them to produce a Christian copy of secular ideas—we could create Parents without Partners for Jesus, Mothers against Drunk Drivers for Jesus (MADDFJ), League of Young Republicans for Jesus, and so on.

When Robert Schuller decided to start his church in Garden Grove, California, he went door-to-door asking people what kind of church they wanted to attend, and on the basis of the responses, he eventually built the Crystal Cathedral. I've always wondered, if Paul had gone door-to-door in Rome and asked those same questions, would the answer have included gladiatorial combat or lion wrestling? In Dr. Schuller's case it probably included movie stars and popular music.

Did his manner of pursuit infect evangelistic technique for the next fifty years? Yes, for whatever reason, the evangelistic world did emulate his survey, and it did happen at least to some degree. But what were the long-range implications of *secularizing up* to attract a secular world? Schuller is not much of a voice anymore in influencing church growth or even relating to the culture. But the notion he planted caught on, and it lives today more than ever. How do you attract dog lovers to church? You have a blessing of the animals service. How do your relate to cowboys? You create a subculture (cowboy church) in which you allow cowboys to wear ten-gallon hats and spurs to church. How do you attract the rock-and-roll culture? You import lasers and smoke machines. How do you attract football fans? Replace the evening worship or even morning worship with a Super Bowl party.

I remember when I first tried to plant a church, the soccer moms wanted an early Sunday service to allow their little ones to play in Sunday leagues. As a witness to how out of touch we were to the secular culture, a quarrel erupted in the congregation about whether it was okay to schedule our Sunday worship around the soccer league's agenda or if Sunday should be kept for worship alone. We finally arrived at a compromise that said it was all right for soccer moms and dads to miss church whenever "necessary" to honor their soccer obligation. It was only one in a long string of *subtracting religious practice* that bowed to secular convenience. The practice of putting any *squeeze on Jesus* is so common now that no one even brings such bartering to the table.

Quit Painting Christ as the Messianic Marketer

For years I taught pastoral leadership courses in seminaries. During those times it was hard not to forbid my students to read Laurie Beth Jones's business books "written from a spiritual perspective." It wasn't that I had anything against Jones personally; it was just that I got tired of trying to wed Christ to a successful, secular, technocratic Jesus who markets Christ's divine mystique to something with no real spiritual correlation. The subtitle of Ms. Jones's book *Jesus C.E.O.* is, *Using Ancient Wisdom for Visionary Leadership.* Even if Jesus believed this and demonstrated it, he never said it in so many words the way Ms. Jones does. She also says in the opening paragraphs of the book that Jesus said, "So is my word that goes out of my mouth: It will not return to me empty, but will accomplish what I desire and achieve the purpose for which I sent it" (Isa. 55:11).[4] The problem with that is that Jesus did not say it. It was the word of the Lord to Isaiah, eight hundred years earlier.

The constant comparison of Jesus to the Fortune 500 crowd leaves Jones's Jesus a captive in the boardroom with twenty-first-century business moguls looking on and applauding approvingly. Taking one of her Christlike comparisons with the local politicians of today, Jones all but inserts the mayor of New York into the da Vinci painting. "Ed Koch, one of the most re-elected mayors of New York City, used to go around town asking people he met, 'How am I doing?' The folks loved him for it, and many considered his openness to be one of the keys to his popularity."[5] Similarly, on the same page she says Al Neuharth, founder of *USA Today,* is a lot like Jesus. All three of them—Ed, Al, and Laurie—are a lot like Jesus.

This kind of imagery pastes the image of Jesus over anything or any viewpoint you want to sell. Over and over the persona of the Son of God is used to cover anything that needs a spotless reputation for self-promotion.

Conclusion

I've never been a proponent of theocracy, but I would like there to be a unifying of the evangelical viewpoint that says we have one way of living and being—*living in one Christlike mode*. This means that our unifying view would cause us to behave and communicate within a single lifestyle—whether in the church or in the world.

For the past decade I have been lost in an ongoing research of Celtic spirituality. What first drew me to the study was a couple of books: Esther De Waal's *The Celtic Way of Prayer*, and only slightly before that, Thomas Cahill's *How the Irish Saved Civilization*. Then from those books I branched out to many others, including a great deal of Irish poetry. What I noticed was that not only did Esther De Waal speak openly of Christ—which in a way might be expected of her own natural affection for her subject—but so did Thomas Cahill, who is a historian and quite devoted to (and good at) his art. But even the secular poets seemed also to speak as freely of Christ as a parish priest might. Our American poets do not speak as freely and openly of Christ.

This Celtic openness intrigued me so much that I finally reached a conclusion that this world of theirs was unified in a wholesome way. (I've never tried this theory out with genuine Celtic scholars.) If there is not a deep division between the secular and the sacred in Celtic Christendom, I wonder if it goes back to the beginnings of the Christian faith in what we later called the British Isles. There were no buildings; they celebrated the Eucharist in the green woods and fields of Scotland and Ireland. Always outside, they were not then, nor did they ever become, the great cathedral builders of Europe. They never had churches and therefore never had church doors; and church doors, I believe, cut the secular and sacred worlds into two distinct parts. People live and communicate outside the doors in one way and inside the doors in quite another way.

> The natural world was the only world that the Celts knew. We sometimes leave our enclosed world (houses, cars, offices, stores and churches) and go "camping." But the Celts weren't camping. . . . Their intense and natural devotion suggests that the closer we are to nature, the more apt we are to pray. . . . Look, for example, at Israel in Sinai. Their outdoor worship revealed YHWH as the breath of God whose breath or wind (*ruach*) created and threatened. . . . His indisputable power was demonstrated in cobras and earthquakes, hail and fire, quail and tamarack.[6]

While Protestants have heard sermons on how important it is to live the same way whether inside or outside the church, the truth is that even the devout rarely do so. I am not saying that all evangelicals are hypocritical, living a double life—holy inside the church and unholy outside the church. Even so, inside the church we are the redeemed community, studying Scripture, praying, and so forth. Outside the church we are committed to getting on in the world, with all the power pursuits and chasing after all the promotions we can. These things are not wrong, but they seem to require a different kind of life than we pursue inside the church.

PART 7

The Denomination Conglomeration

The image of the local church has taken a beating in recent years. Millions of Americans have turned their back on Christian churches because they believe it is hypocritical for churches to preach love but exhibit rancor and division regarding denominational lines, theological distinctives or ethnic differences. Skeptics that we are, Americans are not about to patronize an institution which appears incapable of living what it preaches.

Confidence in the church as a social institution is declining steadily. For many years, the church stood as the most revered social institution. Today it ranks third or fourth on the list.

George Barna[1]

13. DENOMINATIONAL DYSPEPSIA

More than six in ten Americans age seventy and older (62 percent) are Protestant, but this number is only about four in ten (43 percent) among Americans ages eighteen to twenty-nine. Conversely, young adults ages eighteen to twenty-nine are much more likely than those ages seventy and older to say they are not affiliated with any particular religion (25 percent versus 8 percent). If these generational patterns persist, recent declines in the number of Protestants and growth in the size of the unaffiliated population may continue.[2]

14. BELIEVING TOO LITTLE TOO LATE

Four out of ten Christians (40%) strongly agreed that Satan "is not a living being but is a symbol of evil." An additional two out of ten Christians (19%) said they "agree somewhat" with that perspective. . . . More than one-fifth (22%) strongly agreed that Jesus Christ sinned when He lived on earth, with an additional 17% agreeing somewhat. . . . Much like their perceptions of Satan, most Christians do not believe that the Holy Spirit is a living force, either. Overall, 38% strongly agreed and 20% agreed somewhat that the Holy Spirit is "a symbol of God's power and presence but is not a living entity."

George Barna Group[3]

13

Denominational Dyspepsia

The enemy of real community in the church is our task-oriented and radical individualism.

Klaus Issler[1]

How many people on their deathbed wish they'd spent more time at the office?

Stephen Covey[2]

All American religious denominations grew until the middle of the 1950s, at which time growth stalled and decline began. Part of the vitality these denominations had experienced since the end of the Civil War was due to the fact that they zealously guarded their doctrines and treasured their viewpoints. When I began to pastor in 1956 in Oklahoma, there was on the record books of our church the accounts of several public debates between the Southern Baptists (Hunter Baptist Church of Hunter, Oklahoma, of which I was pastor) and the Disciples of Christ in the same town. Back in those times all denominationalists fiercely enjoyed and debated their differences.

I remember how Baptists always stepped into the dock with fiery passion regarding their position that you don't need to be baptized to go to heaven, holding forth their hero—the dying thief whom Jesus welcomed into paradise with no baptism at all (see Luke 23:39–43).

In a wonderful online article, Beverly Whitaker asked in the title of her piece, "What Church Did Grandpa Attend?" Whatever the answer is, we have now reached an age when grandpas—at least 28 percent of them—have not affiliated steadily with any one denomination but have migrated here and there in their religious experience.[3]

On the other hand, the Disciples of Christ relished their power in pointing out to Baptists that Jesus said, "Whoever believes and is baptized will be saved" (Mark 16:16). In the records of those debates, Baptists gathered on one side of the church and the Disciples on the other. The center aisle that separated them was a kind of carpeted DMZ, across which each side lobbed incendiary doctrinal proof-texts at the other.

These days all differences among denominations seem so trivial that they hardly seem worth mentioning. But debates over doctrine were quite common in the early twentieth century. Each denominational church hired glib and well-trained theologians from among their denominational scholars to debate their views of salvation, baptism, communion, and so on. The gatherings usually opened with prayer but were never pietistic events. They were an odd mixture of spiritual passion and gunpowder.

The debates were always well attended and stirred up the members of the community with doctrinal animosities that lasted for decades once the debates were over. Sometimes the arguments began in the sublime and ended in the ridiculous. I remember one Baptist scholar who preached that women would never be welcomed into Southern Baptist pulpits. He reminded us all that Paul said that all preachers had to be "the husband of one wife" (1 Tim. 3:2 NKJV). "How could a woman ever do that?" he shouted, thumping the pulpit to make his point.

In Jane Austen's novel *Sense and Sensibility*, there is a record of one such debate between an Anglican prelate and the atheist scholars of the day; the report (in the novel) was that "the Atheists were routed!" These debates were of course fictional, but reflecting on the quarrelsome prairie affairs in my own near-frontier Oklahoma, I suspect Ms. Austen had seen these same fiery conflicts in Chawton, where her pastor-father preached and influenced her thinking on the subject.

But by the end of the twentieth century, the pride over doctrinal content had all but completely dissipated. By the close of the 1990s, when asked, "What does it mean to be a Christian?" only 19 percent said, "To accept Jesus Christ as Savior," while 22 percent of Christians didn't know. Another 21 percent said it meant to live differently than other people, 14 percent said to love each other, 11 percent said to go to church, and 10 percent said to be a good person.[4] There was no mention of things like eternal security, salvation by grace through faith, and confession of Christ.

Why has there been such a marked decline in denominational doctrinal content? Who can say exactly? Less than half of all adults attend church on any given Sunday. All we do know is that "loyalty to church as an institution in which we have a personal investment, and which we care about is dropping. . . . Willingness to assume a leadership role in the congregation is declining."[5] Between 1986 and 1990 there was a 10 percent drop in the number of people who referred to themselves as religious, and less than half of all Americans opened the Bible during any given week. Studies show that we are a nation of biblical illiterates.

How Rapid Is Denominational Decline?

In the years between 1990 and 2000, only two churches showed any increase in membership among denominational churches:

175

Southern Baptists grew by 1,600,000 during that decade

Assemblies of God grew by 405,000 during those same years

The rest of the denominations showed marked declines:

Missouri Synod Lutheran declined by 104,000

Evangelical Lutheran declined by 157,000

United Church of Christ declined by 164,000

Disciples of Christ declined by 185,000

Episcopal declined by 460,000

Presbyterian Church, USA, declined by 564,000

United Methodist declined by 708,000

Dinesh D'Sousa says that the rate of decline in the liberal churches is especially alarming:

> The liberal churches are losing members in droves. Once these churches welcomed one in six Americans to their various denominations; now they only take in one in thirty. In 1960 the Presbyterian church had 4.2 million members, now it has 2.4 million. The Episcopal church had 3.4 million, now it has 2.3 million. The United Church of Christ had 2.2 million, now it has 1.3 million.[6]

The Schaeffer Institute has compiled some frightening statistics on the rate of church and denominational decline. "Each year more

---

It is odd to even speak of how many members a particular denomination has, because denominational tallies are in constant flux due to the membership wanderlust that exists from denomination to denomination.

"For most adults, this pattern of disengagement is not merely a temporary phase in which they test the boundaries of independence, but is one that continues deeper into adulthood, with those in their thirties also less likely than older adults to be religiously active."

Barna Newsletter[7]

---

than 4,000 churches close their doors. . . . Similarly every year 2.7 million church members fall into inactivity. Between 1990 and 2000 the total membership of all US protestant denominations declined by nearly five million members or more starkly, 9.5 percent."[8]

Most of this rapid decline has been since 1900. At the beginning of the twentieth century, there was an average of twenty-seven churches per 10,000 people. At the end of the century there were only eleven churches per 10,000 people.[9] I need to clarify whether the churches that are dying are all denominational churches. The answer today is no. But the answer at the beginning of the twentieth century was yes, because at that time almost all churches were denominational. At the end? Not so much. Today many church plants are independent churches, and most of those churches are independent because they think denominational churches are visionless sinkholes of lost vitality.

> Given the declining numbers and closure of churches as compared to new church starts, there should have been over 38,000 new churches commissioned to keep up with the population growth.
>
> Richard Krejcir[10]

I believe there are three reasons that the rate of decline is so extreme. First, these nondenominational churches have enormous vitality at the start, but they often struggle later on because of poor funding. On the other hand, many of the denominational church plants thrive better in the long-run because they are attached to the coffers of their founders. Funding, however, is not the primary reason for decline. The number one reason is a dying vision of what Christ established the church to be.

With the decline of vision is a corollary of that decline: the mission of the church has become anemic. The diminishing response to Christ's mandate to missionize is the second reason for the fast rate of decline. Jesus established the church to fulfill his call, but it has been laid aside in favor of a plethora of programs, which include Bible studies, sports leagues, and fellowship dinners. These do furnish some sociological togetherness but not spiritual vitality.

The third reason has to do with poor internal relationships within the church. Nearly every church growth guru I know says that the reason most people leave the church terminally—never to return to any church ever again—is that they have experienced an emotional injury that is so painful they choose to forever avoid any contact with organized religion.

> Every year 2.7 million church members fall into inactivity. This translates into the realization that people are leaving the church. From our research we have found that they are leaving the churches as hurting and wounded victims—of some kind of abuse, disillusionment, or just plain neglect.
>
> Richard Krejcir[11]

Having experienced it a few times myself, I can say there is a great deal of pain in such abuse. I fully understand the cliché, "Christians shoot their wounded." I suspect that evangelicals are very poor at reaching out to those who have been caught in the gearbox of denominational politics. I have never known any denominational dropout who doesn't bear some deep scars that his or her church didn't help to heal.

Maybe that's alright, because so many are now leaving the church that those who continue going have no real expectations of any redeemed behavior from those who still attend. It is as though we have armored ourselves by being blasé because high expectations create deep wounds.

Most Christians praise Christ's crucifixion but turn from being abused themselves—especially at the hands of their fellow believers. So they add to the decline of their church and denomination by keeping out of harm's way.

Local Church = Little Church = High Visitor Visibility

After serving a wonderful rural parish, I became a church planter in 1961 in a town with a population of about 5,000. Virtually anyone could walk to our church no matter where they lived in that town. This was during my first years out of seminary. Not many did walk, but even those who drove didn't have to spend long in their cars to get there. After that I moved to Omaha, Nebraska, to plant another church. From the very outset of my ministry there, my home and my church were far apart. Virtually no church members lived in the neighborhood around our church; many of them lived on the other side of the city. For the first time I realized that if our church was going to grow, I had to abandon the notion that the neighborhood church, all by itself, had little chance of becoming a large church.

> Two of Lasch's axioms reveal why people are leaving churches:
>
> 1. "In an age of diminishing expectations, the Protestant virtues no longer excite enthusiasm."
> 2. "Self-preservation has replaced self-improvement as the goal of earthly existence."[12]
>
> Most Christians would rather avoid hurt than risk social damage from trying to better themselves.

But Omaha is a Midwest, northern-oriented, nonevangelical city. How does the concept of a large, local church work in the Bible Belt? I have for the past decade and a half lived in Alabama. Alabama is packed with Baptists. The old-timers tell tongue-in-cheek stories that lawmakers in Dixie once had a law that any two Baptist churches could not build less than a half-mile from a liquor store or less than a mile from the next Baptist church. Now, say the old-timers, all that has changed. The law now reads that no two Baptist churches can share the same parking lot or liquor store. The Baptist church we now attend is less than five miles from our home, but we still have to drive past three other Baptist churches to get there.

What is nice about the smaller churches I drive by to get to our large church is that if I walked into any one of them, I would be seen and recognized as the *new guy in church*. This means that small parishes have one great advantage over the large church: they find it easier to see and welcome the stranger in their midst. But for the small-church visitor, something frightening occurs. They feel unsafe and vulnerable because of their high visibility.

Megachurch pastors in general and Bill Hybels in particular have made much of the big church as a place of safety. Bill Hybels says the "big church should be a safe place to hear a dangerous message." And what is it that makes the megachurch safe? Anonymity. People hiding from other people who may in some ways endanger or hurt them. The unsafe place then is the small church, where every person is known and first-time visitors stick out like a sore thumb.

Small churches usually mean *close* churches. They are churches you can get to without driving very far. On the other hand, megachurches serve a wide geographical area. They are more inconvenient, being thought of as generally across the town, city, or metropolis.

Generally speaking, denominations are a collection of local churches, that is, churches that are far more likely to belong to more specific neighborhoods and to be attended by people who live in that neighborhood. In my early affiliation with Baptists, there was a kind of creed that said, "When I relocate to a new neighborhood, I will seek out the nearest church and move my letter—that is, my church membership—there." Ultimately, freeways and automobiles made it possible for denominationalists to think *megachurch*, or *the church I really prefer to attend* more than just the church that is closest to me. But Bill Hybels is somewhat right: anonymous Harry and Sherry feel safe in not being discovered by the other attenders.

But he is wrong to infer that people desire anonymity. All of us are highly communal. We all want to be known and esteemed—maybe even loved—by others. Nothing short of this view can explain reality TV, *American Idol*, and the hundreds of talk shows and interview shows that comprise current television formats.

Denominational Dyspepsia

George Barna says the problems of decline are deep-seated:

> The image of the local church has taken a beating in recent years. Millions of Americans have turned their backs on Christian churches because they believe it is hypocritical for churches to preach love but exhibit rancor and division regarding denominational lines, theological distinctives or ethnic differences. Skeptics that we are, Americans are not about to patronize an institution which appears incapable of living what it preaches.[13]

The odd truth about this is that the contemporary evangelical church has been so secularized that her members feel like they are standing for the truth, when in reality, pursuing truth with any real passion disappeared years ago. The creedal truth of the faith has been replaced by a plethora of politically correct ideas that bear no real resemblance to the "faith which was once for all delivered to the saints" (Jude 1:3 NKJV). While the world still likes Jesus, they don't much care for the secondary values that have replaced him. Evangelical churches have adopted a new credo built out of important stuff, just not confessional stuff.

When I sit in church and endure the congregational announcements, I realize we are suffering from a huge creedal dearth. Most evangelicals don't quote the Apostles' Creed—most of them don't know it. The great doctrines go unmentioned, and the creeds have all been thrown under the nontheological bus. Trinitarianism suffers from this creedal shortfall. So does Christology, the Eucharist, immortality of the soul, and for that matter, often biblical preaching. We may argue that the days of doctrinal debates were quaint or even silly, but let us not forget that those were also the days of great denominational loyalty. Now that loyalty has all but disappeared, and in the process of vanishing it has taken the denominations with it.

Small wonder, then, that the Barna Group laments:

Loyalty to congregations is one of the casualties of young adult-hood: twenty-somethings were nearly 70% more likely than older adults to strongly assert that if they "cannot find a local church that will help them become more like Christ, then they will find people and groups that will, and connect with them instead of a local church."[14]

Conclusion

The denominations have become almost completely beside the point. I remember a tongue-in-cheek definition of the difference among them all: Pentecostals are just Baptists on steroids, Baptists are just Methodists with baptisteries, Methodists are just Presbyterians without a credit score, Presbyterians are just Episcopalians without a prayer book, and Episcopalians are just Presbyterians with a stock portfolio. But the comparison is right on target in this respect: denominations have come to define mystiques more than creeds. Denominations represent how intensely you feel your faith more than what you believe. They all believe the same things about the Trinity, heaven and hell, immortality, the second coming, communion, and so forth. Where they happen to differ is seen as trivial by most. There are no differences in beliefs among denominations important enough to die for. Hence the rise of the independent mind and church softball. Give me space and a warm hand and let's live together.

14

Believing Too Little Too Late

"Do you know about the sin of the desert?"
"No," we replied, wondering.
"The sin of the desert is knowing where to find water
and not telling others."[1]

In the 1980s, Christopher Lasch defined the restless searching that causes nomadic Christians to wander from denomination to denomination. Why are they doing it? They are trying to find some stroking for their need to be noticed or to be in charge of their minimal world. In the last half of the twentieth century, evangelicals vaulted into the search for themselves. In prior times they had looked to the lordship of Christ to satisfy their hunger for the only infallible guide to meaning.

Enter Christian narcissism.

As we said in the last chapter, the abandonment of their previous denominational affiliations was of less consequence to Christians than their need to find a nest of warm acceptance. Why do I say this? Because I have been a part of so many congregations in which everyone seems to be pushing the same pursuit in Christian music, creative writing, or audiovisual careers. There is, of course, nothing wrong with this sort of ambition, but it represents a digression from our mission, our evangelism, and our world ministry that was more popular in a less narcissistic age.

> This self-absorption defines the moral climate of contemporary society. The conquest of nature and the search for new frontiers have given way to the search for self-fulfillment.
>
> Christopher Lasch[2]

Young men and women increasingly are turning away from being pastors. This is related to the difficulty that pastoral ministry presents. There is fear of serving as the head of a church because so few who enter pastoral ministry manage to survive. In the seminary where I have served, less than 20 percent of the students are pursuing pastoral ministry. Ministry is all about relationships, and relationships are the thumbscrews of career satisfaction. People can cause us a great deal of hurt, and it is no wonder Charlie Brown or Lucy or Linus—and ultimately Charles Schulz himself—said, "I love humanity; it's people I can't stand."

Narcissus once again rules and raps the gavel on the ordination of people who love Jesus enough to serve him, but not enough to deal with a life of constant congregational unrest. Lasch once again speaks to this syndrome:

> Arising out of a pervasive dissatisfaction with the quality of personal relations, it advises people not to make too large an investment in love and friendship, to avoid excessive dependence on others, and to live for the moment—the very conditions that created the crisis of personal relations in the first place.[3]

All in all, I suspect the diminishing number of pastors is occurring mainly within the dying of evangelicalism. For most of these, the oft-ignored Apostles' Creed has been replaced by a fearful motto: I don't want to get hurt, so *don't nobody bring me no bad news.*

Unfortunately, ever since the Colosseum was built, Christians have been getting hurt. Remember Hybels said that the megachurch must be a safe place to hear a dangerous message? A small church may be an especially dangerous place to hear a safe message. Why is it dangerous? Well it is dangerous because every arena of relationship causes danger. Just as you can get hurt in a board meeting at GM or the PTA meeting in Harper Valley, you can be seriously and emotionally injured in a Baptist business meeting. The major difference lies in where you get hurt. If you are hurt in the corporate structure, you lick your wounds and keep on working until you get your gold watch at sixty-five years. If you get hurt at the PTA, you can drop out or homeschool your kids. But if you get hurt at church, your bitterness eats at your joy for years to come.

My book *The Singer* was published thirty-seven years ago, and it depicts Christ as being crushed in the heavy gears of mechanistic religion. Denominations grow heavy with bureaus and commissions. The creativity these denominations once welcomed and cherished has been jettisoned just to keep the heavy wheels running. Big churches require big government and steal liberty. Entropy wins at last as the machine begins to slog down with dull business.

> **Syllogism**
> Major Premise: God is a custom.
> Minor Premise: A custom is an old, old habit.
> Conclusion: God is an old, old habit.[4]

The machine was always evangelistic and once produced new adherents apace. During its vital days it rehearsed its commission to evangelize and wept at altars of passion. But in time, the passion died and the altars grew dry as the Sahara. The fiery sermons and prophecies became shibboleths of death.

We finally quit saying the words and came to believe that to say the words was to ask for the lies they implied. In the case of us Baptists, we never quit singing "Just as I Am." But after a while it occurred to us that we had stayed "just as we were" too. Why are big churches safe? Because they are program and activity centered,

> Even invitations can become the dullest part
> of our dull religious habits. In my book on
> preaching, I rephrased "Just as I Am" this way:
>
> > Just as I am without one plea.
> > I've come to sign form one-oh-three,
> > That the church clerk just handed me.
> > I understand the lunch is free,
> > O Lamb of God I come.[5]

and they increasingly trade missions and evangelism for stodgy, sometimes boring programs. There is less hurt in boredom than in passion. So to avoid the pain, we trade in our bright faith for dull creeds. Unwittingly, however, stodginess kills life-giving passion. Stodginess also throws the kingdom of God into decline.

We have lost so much passion that we have arrived at the edges of our continuance; we can't decline any further. People will forgive any shortcoming about any organization except a lack of passion. Traditional churches often have quartered themselves in tasteless temples to practice their stale religion. Disconnected Christians seldom quit believing in God, but they do quit believing in the church where they ceased to find any meaningful trace of God's reality.

Evangelicals Die When They Believe Too Little to Live

To begin this section, I want to call to mind the theological atmosphere at the start of the twentieth century. Fundamentalism rose in protest to the progressive movement of that day. There was a huge optimism in the year 1900. So many scientific marvels had been accomplished in the closing years of the nineteenth century that it seemed as though there was a bright new hope that the kingdom of heaven was being born before the very eyes of the theological community. Diseases were disappearing; life spans were

> Thou waitest for a spark from heaven, and we,
> Light half-believers of our casual creeds,
> Who never deeply felt, nor clearly willed . . .
> Who hesitate and falter life away,
> And lose tomorrow the ground won today.
>
> Matthew Arnold (1822–1888)[6]

increasing; science was offering the world a century of new hope. There was no significant war at the turn of the last century; the battlefields of the day had been plowed up and sown as grain fields. All of this seemed to be ushering in a kingdom of peace. Within little more than a decade, however, the entire world was engulfed in a multinational conflict, only to see the process repeated a scant two decades later.

Fundamentalism rose to correct the bright, new, humanist-driven notion that contentious religion was an old and useless idea that the bright, new world could live without. People seemed to have outgrown their old religious impediments, but the outcry of the fundamentalists grew stern in preaching a return to the fundamentals of biblical faith. The list of things fundamentalists championed sounds very much like the list that evangelicals later came to preach and believe.

> In a Barna Group survey, being an "evangelical" was described as "believing they have a personal responsibility to share their religious beliefs about Christ with non-Christians; believing that Satan exists; believing that eternal salvation is possible only through grace, not works; believing that Jesus Christ lived a sinless life on earth; asserting that the Bible is accurate in all that it teaches; and describing God as the all-knowing, all-powerful, perfect deity who created the universe and still rules it today."[7]

The doctrinal aspects of fundamentalism soon gave way to more social, nonbiblical beliefs like the evils of drinking alcohol, smoking cigarettes, chewing tobacco, dipping snuff, playing cards, going to a movie theater, and in some cases—for women—the evils of cosmetics, bobbed hair, jewelry, shorts, slacks, and divorce. These lists were soon expanded to include pool halls, gambling, racetracks, magazines, and novels.

There can be little doubt that the fundamentalists meant well. They initially hoped to purify and redefine Christian theology. They ended up sewing so many new patches on old theological garments that the new theological fabric of their beliefs was lost in legalisms.

So much for life on the right end of things; but on the left end of things, the liberals fared little better. Schleiermacher had led European theologians far afield from seeing the Bible as the basis for a reasonable Christian faith. Karl Barth, trying to minister to his war-torn parish in Safenwil, said he found the scriptural weakness of European liberals gave him too little substance to preach to his needy church. He saw the liberalism of the day as too anemic to offer the broken souls of his World War I parish. His reply of strength to these flimsy theologians was his 1919 publication of *Romerbrief*, a theological commentary on the book of Romans. He eventually succeeded in moving the German church (and ultimately all Western faith) back to a biblical foundation.

> "Born again Christians" are defined as people who said they have made a personal commitment to Jesus Christ that is still important in their lives today and who also indicated that they believe that when they die they will go to heaven because they had confessed their sins and had accepted Jesus Christ as their savior.
>
> Barna Group[8]

Between Barth and the spirited evangelical movement that grew out of fundamentalism came a new hope for the world. Ultimately, evangelicalism would surpass the Barthian revival in fervor and numerical growth. The glory of its passion and missiology was fiery and effective for many decades. It was only in the last two or three decades that evangelicalism began to crack its once-towering structure and fracture its foundations.

These fractures did not come primarily because of evangelical theologians, who, while not always agreeing with each other, seemed generally to tolerate and even appreciate all their differences. Where then did these foundational fissures come from? They arose from the new church laity, whose famous pastors (often megachurch pastors) bore separatist theological differences that became intolerable to each other. The fissures first appeared among people like Norman Vincent Peale and certain denominational large-church pastors, particularly in southern churches. There was a feeling that Schuller on the West Coast and Peale on the East Coast were preaching cheap grace and easy *gospelism*. It smacked so much of heresy that these large-church pastors held little in common with their peers. Innumerable quarrels broke out among many large-church pastors, who disagreed over Calvinism, the existence and nature of hell, and various aspects of prophecy. These pastors had vital congregations who, like themselves, held passionately to their viewpoints. But generally, these pastors lacked the theological know-how to help evangelicalism move into the future with a thoughtful, studied foundation.

The Stranglehold of Anticultural Traditionalists

The church growth end of evangelicalism, dominated by its own zeal, collected a few (comparatively speaking) churches that became more preoccupied with getting bigger than going deeper. This movement fed on an almost entirely suburban sociology and soon began to show signs of dumbing down. Its methodology of growth was programs-a-go-go. The evangelistic heart of late-twentieth-century gurus like D. James Kennedy or Bill Bright was replaced by a thousand lifestyle evangelistic programs, which for all its seemingly easy, chatty ideas about personal evangelism, often dissipated into happy conversations that were cheerful but powerless.

"Witnessing to Win" programs within all denominations replaced the word *witness* with the word *outreach*, which had a more nebulous, less biblical-sounding definition, making it less scary. Meanwhile, the internet and cable religious programming joined the megachurch in an abundance of new forms of study groups that led its adherents to be even more shallow. Then with the nineties began the massive abandonment of church attendance.

Further, as the more traditional churches ceased to cherish their traditions, they seemed unable to find themselves. Dinesh D'Sousa, however, cited Southern Baptists as evidence that denominational churches were growing: "The traditional churches, not the liberal churches, are growing in America. In 1960, for example, the churches affiliated with the Southern Baptist Convention had 8.7 million members. Now they have 16.4 million."[9] But is the denomination really growing as D'Sousa suggests? Its denominational growth began to slow in the 1980s

> The denomination must now decide whether it cares more about its past heritage or its future vitality.
>
> Jonathan Merritt[10]

and '90s and continued to show declines in the new millennium. Southern Baptists may not be in as marked a decline as Methodists, for instance, but the trend lines are certainly present.

Southern Baptists are currently struggling again with whether to change their name. They have voted on this eight times since 1965, and each time the motion has failed. Part of the problem is that the denomination has often not attracted new adherents because of the name. I can speak with experience here.

I planted a Southern Baptist church in Omaha in 1966 and remained its pastor until 1991. I loved and still love my denomination, but it became clear to me that if the church was to grow by attracting non–Southern Baptists to its membership, we would have to play down the geographical adjective. In the case of our church, we ultimately began referring to the church as simply Westside Church, dropping the other two adjectives that people generally found unappealing: *Southern* and *Baptist* both had to go.

Almost all current denominations seem to be anticultural. Since 1960 Methodists have lost nearly half of their membership, which some people feel is due in part to their position against the ordination of gays. This goes for a lot of other denominations as well. Jonathan Merritt, a fine young Baptist scholar, pointed out that Southern Baptists even got in trouble with Mickey Mouse. "In the past the Southern Baptist Convention has been a magnet of controversy. From boycotting Walt Disney's 'pro-gay stances' to a perceived near alignment with the Republican Party, it always seemed to play the role of crusader."[12]

> A 2006 Center for Missional Research/Zogby poll found that many Americans have a negative impression of the denomination. More than 40 percent of eighteen- to twenty-four-year-olds said knowing a church was Southern Baptist would negatively affect their decision to visit or join.
>
> Jonathan Merritt[11]

Conclusion

What is the summation of the denominational milieu at the beginning of the third millennium? There is no easy way to sketch it out and no easy panacea to cure our ills. But as Douglas MacArthur said at the Japanese surrender on the deck of the battleship *Missouri*, "We have had our last chance. . . . It must be of the spirit if we are to save the flesh." And so it will be. In the final chapters of this book, I sketch a plan for individual survival. I say *individual* because I hold not the slightest hope for the triumph of the entire faith.

The ways of God, it seems to me, first created various denominations around a glorious dream of world redemption. In time, that dream became encrusted with calcified bureaus and a lot of good ideas that were hatched in boardrooms rather than in the throes of wind-and-fire revivals.

And so it came to pass, that when the good ideas became too leaden to fly, we tried in vain to make them work anyway.

I have said repeatedly in this book that there are no pendulums. I believe we can hold out little hope of simply swinging back to vitality. Even so, who knows but that in some upper room, just after the Eucharist, the wind will blow again, and in that isolated moment we never expected will come a new Pentecost. Even if it is far away from our tall glass buildings and our long mahogany tables, do not despise the flame. Run headlong and jump into the fire!

And if it never happens in a place where you can discover it, determine you will be the lover—the last lover, if necessary—to cry out and wait for his coming. It is always the unexpected little moments that hide what ceased to occur in denominational boardrooms: a real fire born in a little moment. For if institutions cannot be saved, may his isolated lovers find what the institutions missed: a partner on the road to Emmaus where our hearts burn within us. Who knew the fire was there?

PART 8

A Recovery of Passion and Discipline

My son, the more thou canst go out of thyself,
    so much the more wilt thou be able to enter into Me.
As to be void of all desire of external things, produceth inward
    peace,
    so the forsaking of ourselves inwardly, joineth us unto God.
I will have thee learn perfect renunciation of thyself to My will,
    without contradiction or complaint.
Follow thou Me: "I am the Way, the Truth and the Life,"
    Without the Way there is no going,
    Without the Truth there is no knowing;
    Without the Life there is no living.
I am the Way thou oughtest to follow,
    the Truth thou oughtest to trust;
    the Life which thou oughtest to hope for.
I am the inviolable Way, the infallible Truth, the endless Life.
    and the truth that shall make thee free.

                     Thomas à Kempis, *The Imitation of Christ*

15. THE SEARCH FOR PASSION AND DISCIPLINE

The church in the West is struggling to connect with the next generation. We are dealing with the immense theological, spiritual and social changes that define our times. . . . How can we prepare the next generation to live meaningfully and follow Jesus wholeheartedly in these changing times? . . . The Christian community needs a new mind—a new way of thinking, a new way of relating, a new vision of our role in the world—to pass on the faith to this and future generations.

David Kinnaman[1]

16. BUILDING A LIVING ARMY IN A VALLEY OF DRY BONES

Many of the assumptions on which we have built our work with young people are rooted in modern, mechanistic, and mass production paradigms. Some (though not all) ministries have taken cues from the assembly line, doing everything possible to streamline the manufacture of shiny new Jesus-followers, fresh from the factory floor. But disciples cannot be mass-produced. Disciples are handmade one relationship at a time.

David Kinnaman[2]

15

The Search for Passion and Discipline

For the first heaven, Christ showed me his Father, not
in any bodily likeness but in his attributes and in his
operations. That is to say, I saw in Christ that the Father
is. For the Father's operation is this: He rewards his
son Jesus Christ.

For he is well pleased with all the deeds that Jesus
has done for our salvation; and therefore we are his, not
only through our redemption, but also by his Father's
courteous gift. We are his bliss, we are his reward, we
are his honor, we are his crown.

Julian of Norwich[1]

If there are no pendulums, and the health of our faith will never
swing back to its former vitality, how do we fight for our continual
right in the future to enjoy our faith? To begin with, the crusade
to save the movement must start with zeal to save ourselves. It has

been an ever-circling prayer of evangelicals to *pray up* a worldwide revival and try with such a spiritual firestorm to see all our lost ground regained at once. Our same desire for revival has been the goal of Catholic missionaries across the ages as well; *Ignem Mitterre in Terram* (cast fire upon the earth) is the motto of the Society of Jesus (Jesuits). In every evangelical church in which I've worshiped, they have kept this prayer front and center in their worship and practice. But in the little Pentecostal church I attended as a child, we sang a hymn whose final line was: *Lord, send a revival and let it begin with me.*

The Revival of the Church Is a One-at-a-Time Revival

This book describes that longing as a sign that the church is well as long as it *dreams of and prays for revival*. But it is more than that; it is a cry to see an eroding evangelicalism as enduring. Our fullest hope is that there is much that can be done to keep the further erosion of the movement in a state of remission. It is to that hope that I address these final chapters. But to try to preserve the movement in its entirety is pointless. We must make the starting point of our reform ourselves. Each of us—one by one—must seek our own individual vitality. The way to save the whole is, as it has always been, to focus on the parts.

This has been a growing conviction of mine as I have watched American evangelicalism stagnate as it slipped from its once rapid-growth posture into the same pattern of atrophy that has plagued other religious movements. I have watched my own denomination try to drum up a revival of our own with mere programs and slogans; all to no avail. Now it seems we have lost our grip on the ascent and are slowly slipping backward. It is painful to watch, and I'm not sure we have reached the point of realizing that we cannot save our denomination by simply whomping up a battery of new programs centered on evangelism and outreach. We have already sewn too many hopeful patches on a very old garment.

This same realization came to George Barna, and his general message has been tailored to call all evangelicals to approach the slide with an emphasis on individual vitality, which may or may not ever add up to corporate vitality. But it is our fondest hope.

Dropping the Every-Church-a-Megachurch Madness

As a first step to this goal, I believe that each pastor must drop the insulin-driven drive to make each church bigger. In my years as a cleric, I have too often served the demon of pastoral competition and watched him destroy fine young men who finally collapsed in fatigue because they couldn't make it happen.

It is time to trade this bogus yearning into an honest effort to quit bullying our churches to try to become the biggest and the best on our block or in

> I came to realize that a nation, a culture, or even a local community isn't changed all at once. If we're alert and prepared, we may get the privilege of participating in the reconstruction of one other life. In the end, those humble efforts may add up to a revolution, or they may not; but when we're realistic about what can happen through our efforts, the big trends are no longer overwhelming and depressing. They are simply new opportunities to be mastered so that we can change the world for Christ, one life at a time.
>
> George Barna[2]

our city. We do not need to be number one! Perhaps it is time to throw away all the church growth books that have held us captive to this hellish ego-dream. Most talk of getting bigger only keeps us from getting better and loving higher. Let every day begin not with celebrating our schedule but with clinging to his love. Let St. John of the Cross call you back to the only verity that must stand at the center of your sanity: the love of the Father.

My soul is occupied
And all my substance is in his service.
Now I guard no flock,
Nor have I other employment,
My sole occupation is love.
   Before the soul succeeded in effecting
This gift and surrender of itself to the beloved,
It was entangled in many useless occupations
   by which it sought to please itself and others.
All this is over now—
For all its thoughts, words and action
Are directed to God.
   All my occupation now is the practice
Of the love of God.
All I do is done in Love.

                St. John of the Cross[3]

Then, for all of the members, taken individually, we should each develop our own individual commitment to the spiritual disciplines. To begin with, we need to pray and read the Bible (better yet, study the Bible) with pen in hand and paper in front of us so we can keep a journal in which we reflect on his glory.

Do not keep this journal too near your calendar, for it may be your calendar that has kept you checking slots and writing in things to do. Let your journal teach you that *what you need to be* is more important than *what you need to do*. Start by spending at least ten minutes reading the Scriptures aloud in prayer—*praying the Scriptures*. Read systematically through the book of Psalms, at least one psalm a day. Keep a hymnal close at hand and read at least one hymn a day. Teach your soul to sing; you may have been running so fast for God that you whizzed by the better music. Only a sturdy song can heal the tuneless sickness in our competitive spirits. We will never be healed by anything less than a recovery of that endless inner celebration that swabs the tuneless monotony from the center of our souls.

Coming Home to the Spiritual Disciplines

Chief among the virtues that produce vitality is the discipline of ministry. Investigate the ways your church cares for souls and find out how to make them ever more effective. Mother Teresa said it is never good to keep our hands so folded in prayer we cannot open them to serve. Serving others is the only way to complete your identity in Christ. If you only celebrate Jesus, you will only be a celebrator, but the moment you touch someone in his name, you become Jesus for that person. You are the human agent who says to anyone you touch, "Heaven is closer than you think, and God is more accessible than you have dreamed."

In the final chapter we will deal with those confessional values that are rooted in the creeds and covenants. But to arrive at revitalized faith, we must find a grand vitality in worship. To do that you must develop your own liturgy. Read the Apostles' Creed at the beginning of each of your devotional exercises; no matter how long you spend each day and no matter for how long you focus on the disciplines, always start your day affirming what you already believe about God and his Son. "I believe in God the Father Almighty, maker of heaven and earth." As you read or quote this statement of faith, you will develop the habit of the faith affirmation in your heart. Never grow weary of its truth.

While I will deal with this subject in the final chapter, for the moment let me emphasize the discovery of reading the lives and thoughts of Christianity's mystics and martyrs. This is one of the richest of all exercises. I have gained years of blessings by reading the works of those, my long-ago brothers and sisters. These gallant disciples loved Christ and wrote all they felt, until their lives were merged with his—union with Christ—in a glorious oneness. I know these were my brothers and sisters in another day, and as sure as Thérèse of Lisieux lived, I shall be in her company one day as well as the company of Teresa of Avila and Mother Teresa of

Calcutta. These are sisters of mine who make me wealthy because they walked with Christ. I must read them so that I may allow them to lead me to God.

Needless to say, it is all-important to find the support of a real community of faith; get in touch with a congregation in which the preaching and teaching are closely tied to Scripture. I know of no other way to say it: we must hear the word preached, and it must be *a* word filled with *the* Word.

It is not surprising that this simple admonition is going to be increasingly difficult to fulfill. Gradually, faith in the Bible has been eroding during the past four decades.

> In a time of universal deceit, telling the truth is a revolutionary act.
>
> George Orwell[4]

Only if we hear the Bible faithfully preached can we find the footing we need to stand. We are, after all, the revolutionaries of the kingdom. We cannot stand unless we hear it preached by someone who believes it—who burns with fire and yet bleeds to heal the broken to whom he preaches.

Seeking Passion

Authentic passion is not a value to be driven for too directly. One doesn't get it because he or she goes out looking for it. Passion is the result of coming into the embrace of a loving God. When the embrace of God is all-encompassing, a passion for divine love is born. Other things are also born: the evangelism of Acts 2 is set loose and church growth occurs. But these things, like passion itself, are not the goal of life. They are but by-products of our craving for God.

Beware lest you become obsessed with making the church bigger rather than making God bigger. Years ago I listened to J. B. Phillips remind me that my God was too small. I sometimes feel that we are haunted by a million experts helping us make the churches ever bigger with a God who is too small. We were never called to build big churches. That was to be the consequence of our God-love and Christ-obedience. We were called to create in the middle of our pursuit of Christ a space big enough for a very large God. If the church got big, it would be because we were long-suffering enough to wait for him to tamper with its size. God makes small churches larger in the simple act of filling them with himself. Anything else is growth by gimmickry.

> It appears that the strategy of Christ was to win the loyalty of the few who would honestly respond to the way of living. They would be the pioneers of the new order, the spearhead of the advance against mass ignorance, selfishness, evil, "play acting," and apathy of the majority of the human race.
>
> J. B. Phillips[5]

Avoiding Gaudy Conversionism

A healthy, growing church is not a matter of setting numerical goals. Churches grow as we desire the nearness of God. Lots of things (that have very little to do with God) can make churches get bigger, including creative leadership or a simple surge of population demographics.

If there's any doubt that we are doing anything wrong by being part of a gaudy conversionist drive to make every church in America grow, we have but to ask ourselves why we are working so hard at evangelism if the effort is producing only denominational decline and evangelical death. The most obvious answer to that question is that we have conditioned ourselves from the onset of the church growth movement to push, push, push for converts. As Jesus said to the Pharisees, "You travel land and sea to win one proselyte, and when he is won, you make him twice as much a son of hell as yourselves" (Matt. 23:15 NKJV).

The young devotees of most church growth gurus do not want to be anointed so they can be like Christ; they only want to be like their fair-haired icons of church growth success. This is achieved by mimicking popular tastes and cultural trends. Currently the costume of church planting is done by dressing like rock stars rather than nineteenth-century bankers. In their estimations, a trap-set is more central to success than serving the heartbeat of the Gospel of John.

> In the optimistic mid-periods between world wars, some Christians talk brightly of the "earth being filled with the knowledge of the Lord as the waters cover the sea" and of "the Kingdoms of this world becoming the Kingdom of our God and of His Christ"—as though the world-wide acceptance of the reign of God were just around the corner. This is, of course, nonsense. Those who respond to the Truth have always been a minority.
>
> J. B. Phillips[6]

The disease is widespread. The degeneration of our motives is easily spotted. But with each successive decade of pushing to grow bigger churches, there have been less and less converts. Now there is only a trickle of real disciples. The movement dwindles, but the dwindling has not diminished our push to make things work out. We have misunderstood: Jesus didn't found a mass movement; he founded a minority movement that set out to avoid the wide turnpikes of success because his way was one made narrow with spiritual disciplines (Matt. 7:14).

Any sweeping response to Jesus when he was on earth was not overly large. There were, after all, only 120 people in the upper room who awaited the coming of the Spirit and the birth of the church.

> Indeed it would appear that Christ (knowing how firmly evil and selfishness are entrenched and how hard it is for men to break away from their own self-love) did not anticipate a full-scale establishing of God's Kingdom on this planet. . . .
>
> The follower of the new way is therefore called to do all he can to spread "the good news of the Kingdom," but to realize at all times that the success or failure of the Kingdom can never be judged by

a simple reference to statistics of [church growth] "Christians" at any particular time.[7]

Ego calls us to tout our success. The Spirit bids us seek only wind and flame.

The best methodologies do in time die. The Spirit bids us seek only the wind and flame.

How-to books are only ink and paper. Pentecost lives forever.

What Does Being *Anointed* Really Mean?

One of my favorite maxims is, "When the horse is dead, dismount!" I believe the church-growth-by-goal-setting horse is dead. As we have said earlier in the book, it is not dead everywhere in the world, only in the West. The problem with the *let's get bigger* push is that it is tied to our idea of success and gross-national-product conversionism. This drive has gotten all scrambled together with such spiritual concepts as *the anointing*.

I recently spoke to a group of 150 young men and women who had surrendered themselves to the gospel ministry. Prior to my time with them, they had visited a megachurch. This church has a highly motivated pastor who is becoming something of a legend in our city. The thousands who attend there have been challenged by the pastor's very popular books. He is a fiery preacher and stirs his congregation to be ever more involved in missions and personal evangelism. One of the students in the group asked me if I believed in "the anointing."

Not knowing where his query was headed, I said cautiously, "Yes, of course. There are those throughout history who have had the anointing, and God seems to have given them an extra measure of grace and influence in his church."

Then the questions grew specific. "Do you believe this Dixie megachurch pastor, who has vaulted so suddenly into prominence, is anointed?"

I said that it seems that he is.

"Why are you so hesitant to proclaim his anointing?"

"I am not hesitant," I said, "but a big church alone is not the evidence of the anointing. There are huge churches driven by the current success syndrome where few, if any, real kingdom principles can be found."

"But *bigness* must be a sign of the anointing," one of them said. "Numbers matter."

"Crooks attended Jesus wherever he went, but they also followed Genghis Khan. By your logic, Benny Hinn, Joel Osteen, and Joyce Meyer must also be anointed," I said, "for they have millions who attend their services. On the other hand, Adoniram Judson worked for seven years in India before he ever made a single convert." I continued, "Who would say he was not anointed? For that matter, there are many evidences that the apostle Paul never pastored or even founded a large church. There are no evidences that Paul ever preached to huge crowds like Peter or Apollos. Was he anointed?"

> Our union with Christ is both the prize of our passion and the trophy of his resurrection. What can it mean to speak of his suffering as the prize? Just this: If ever you are prone to doubt that Christ loves you, simply ask him for the evidence. He will show you his scars and say, "These I had in loving you. I beg you to enter into my wounds and find our union all that both of us desire."[8]

"But this church's founding pastor has written religious best sellers," said the student.

"So have Benny Hinn, Joel Osteen, and Joyce Meyer," I replied.

"But . . . but . . . but. . . ."

"Listen, I'm not arguing for or against the anointed status of your hero or any of the other cable personalities. In fact, purely from my observation, I believe your candidate for being labeled as 'anointed' has a better shot at the title than many other claimants. But there is in the anointing something far beyond just having a big church. An anointed man or woman is one who has an affair with God, who adores the indwelling Spirit, and who is lost in the rich fortune of grace. His constant thoughts are about God. His constant goal is his own momentary obedience. He longs for the second coming of Jesus and a face-to-face experience with Christ."

"Well," the student said, "our hero is electric in spirit; he has every virtue you have named."

"Then," I said, "he is unquestionably anointed."

For the moment the matter was settled. Right then and there we proclaimed their candidate for the title to be anointed. The students were happy with the annunciation, and so, for that matter, was I. In his case, however, I feel the students were more convinced by his popular success than they were by my suggestions of his Christ-compulsion.

I believe one who is possessed by this *divine romance* will speak of Jesus as lovers speak of each other. I believe there will reside in such a one a summons to adoration as a lover of Christ. I believe such a one can be hushed to reverence by the sweetness of his name. For our age, the state of evangelicals is dying. We are, by our president's own confession, a nation of many nonbelievers. Unbelief—as always—is the real sin of the day. In this tough environment, I know what heartache lies in young pastors who are

> In June of 2007, then Senator Barack Obama told CBS news: "Whatever we once were, we're no longer a Christian nation. At least not just. We are also a Jewish nation, a Muslim nation, a Buddhist nation, a Hindu nation, and a nation of non-believers."[9]

encouraged to have an anointed ministry that never comes to them. There are, as we have said, approximately 1,500 megachurches in the United States. There are 45,000 seminary students and 340,000 churches. Only .003 percent are going to wind up with a big church.

If I were God—and I often play this mental game to help me understand the world situation—would I call all of these pastors and only anoint .003 percent of them? No, I would give freely of my Spirit to all those who crave holiness. If I were God, I would give myself freely to those who serve their most ardent desire for me. These I would anoint. If I were God, I would exalt every saint who practices the art of divine love. I would start evangelizing the world by anointing those who hunger for obedience. The power of transformation I would give to those who satisfy the heart of divine love. Only then would I anoint them. It would not be those who strive to grow a church but those who hunger for God's pleasure. These I would bless first, whatever the size of the church.

The Marriage of Spiritual Passion and the Spiritual Disciplines

The queen of all the disciplines is prayer. Prayer is both the armor and the weapon of the believer. William Cowper thought of prayer as Satan's terror. There is a thoughtful wonder in writing your prayers. Once the haphazardness of extempore is gone, prayers grow to a kind of celebration. This is particularly true of journaling when you reflect on his glory in a precise way, pen in hand.

If prayer is the queen of the disciplines, perhaps we need to consider evangelism as the most valorous. It is the discipline that requires courage above all. So far in my church experience, I have noticed that congregations who really emphasize soul winning promote it as one of the many program offerings that the church emphasizes. But taken with all that is offered, it appears only as one more kind of calendar congestion. Even so, it is a noble congestion because it is the last command of Christ for his church.

> Restraining prayer we cease to fight;
> Prayer makes the Christian's armor bright,
> And Satan trembles when he sees
> The weakest saint upon his knees.
>
> William Cowper[10]

Evangelism is rarely a popular program in the church because the average layperson sees it as terrifying work and therefore chooses nursery work or the flower committee as a timid alternative. Not that they take up much of the work of spiritual formation either. Prayer and Bible study are seen as laborious and maybe even tedious. Hospital ministry is nearly as fearsome as going into the neighborhood to call on homes, where the anxiety they face is all the more frightening.

I have never met a person who turned to the disciplines because he or she found them easy or safe, at least at first. Thomas à Kempis thought of the disciplines as the hard "work of the interior." The word *discipline* is related to the word *disciple*, which in its Latin root means "student." Why is being a student so hard? Because students study. Disciples study the teachings of their master, and their master—if he is a good master—requires much of his students. He asks them to read, write papers, create documents, learn footnoting, produce essays, and develop arguments.

> The devil is outrageous only against prayer, and those who exercise it; because he knows it is the true means of taking his prey from him. . . . No sooner does one enter into a spiritual life, a life of prayer, but they must prepare for strange crosses. All manner of persecutions and contempts in this world are reserved for that life.
>
> Madame Guyon[11]

I have taught in a seminary for more than twenty years, and I have hardly ever found a student who really enjoyed the discipline of his or her studies. I often hear students carping about how hard the course is. I hear them say, "Prof, do we really need to study the messianic consciousness? Why? Couldn't we just talk about Jesus and how wonderful he is? Couldn't we just give our testimony and not have to read and write any more papers? We just want to *feel* his love, not search through books to try to understand the New Testament."

> Lament thou and grieve, that thou art yet so carnal. . . . So unwatchful over thy outward senses, so often entangled with so many vain fancies: So much inclined to outward things, so negligent in the interior: So prone to laughter and immodesty, so indisposed to tears and compunction. . . . So covetous of abundance, so sparing in giving. . . . So wakeful to hear gossiping tales, so drowsy at sacred services: So hasty to arrive at the end thereof, so inclined to be wandering and inattentive: So negligent in the prayers, so lukewarm in celebrating the holy eucharist . . . So quickly distracted, so seldom wholly gathered into thyself.
>
> Thomas à Kempis[12]

The Recovery of an Honest Evangelism

Evangelism itself, however, has two strikes against it. First, it is the most obnoxious of the disciplines because it is the most frightening. There is almost nothing more scary, for instance, than standing at a doorbell with the courageous intention of actually ringing it. The finger weighs a thousand pounds as it reaches for the tiny pearl button of a doorbell. And since the demise of the screen door, heavy front doors open too suddenly, and the all-at-once-ness of a door swinging open is a kind of sociological purgatory. The old camaraderie of "Hello there!" has been replaced by the unspoken reprimand, "Who the hell are you?" Politicians do it and political supporters do it. Charitable canvassers and life-and-death fund-raisers do it. Mormons do it and the Jehovah's Witnesses do it, but hardly any evangelicals ever do it. Many megachurch pastors actually teach against it.

The garage door opener is the last line of defense. This is defiant sociology that threatens our witness. On Friday night it clicks our car into a world of seclusion, swallowing it whole just before the evening news, and the sanctity of the unevangelized home is secured. Beyond the garage door is the great suburban hiding place.

There we hide our bodies and plug our ears, and all the time God is calling, calling. Calling what? Calling, "Receive me. I am come that you may have life."

Praise be to the garage door opener. It will click us back out into the traffic on Monday morning, and between the clicks, let no invader crash the gates of our privacy even under the guise of trying to keep us out of hell. Fifty years ago *keeping the world out of hell* was a noble goal. But these days it is not regarded as all that important. Nobody really believes in hell anymore, and so keeping people out of it is a concern the church has even lately laid aside.

The interesting corollary to hell—the doctrine of heaven—has gotten increasingly spongy too. Heaven, by comparison to hell, has been a more pleasant doctrine, but while most people believe in it, it has a gelatinous framework that Randy Alcorn has come closest to getting right.[14] Just how gelatinous is obvious in the myriad books retelling people's trips to heaven and back again. Indeed it seems more and more publishers, realizing how much money they were losing by not getting the contract on the most popular of these, have managed to find still more people who went to heaven and have joined the race for book contracts on these stories. But wait, there's more. Now hell also has had an evangelical visitor who, not to be outdone, has also come back with a book contract. But none of these experiential theologians have arrested the endless conjecturing of what heaven may really be like.

So with a hell that nobody wants and a heaven that is so ill-defined, our goals are befuddled. Evangelicals don't have a hell to save people from or a concrete heaven to lead people to.

> I am the lover of purity and the giver of all sanctity. I seek a pure heart, and there is my place of rest. Make ready for me a large upper room furnished, and I will keep the Passover at thy house. . . . I am he that have called thee, I have commanded it to be done, I will supply what is wanting in thee; come thou and receive me.
>
> Thomas à Kempis[13]

But the big deterrent to door-to-door evangelism is of little interest to comfortable suburbanites, who are locked in man-caves and home theaters, and just don't want to be disturbed. Aside from the taboo of privacy invasion that none of us much care for, the greatest emphasis of the pampered democracy is that the two steps between the threshold and the doorbell is the DMZ, with signs that say, "Come no closer. I am a member of the comfortable society, and I am exceedingly *uncomfortable* with you on my doorstep. I would be even more uncomfortable if you were actually in my house. So go away."

> Evangelism is the art of speaking about things transcendent and having the here-and-now world tolerate us—even more, of speaking about all our obligations to God and having them adore us. Yet it is the first work of God to light the exits for the fire that's on the way. It is desperate work, but properly seen, there is joy in the desperation.

And for those who hold any hope of converting their friends in the company lunchroom, the corporate boardroom, or any popular bistro, the comfort index rules. Our Western world has walked away from the necessity of God, and the matter is closed.

Conclusion

The world is no longer standing on tiptoe waiting to hear what the people who believe nothing have to say. Those people who believe nothing have become purveyors of luncheons and softball and get-a-date dot-com. Every year our lack of content and our loss of passion only add to our statistics of decline.

Not much is needed to reverse things. We only need to have the old Samaritan divorcee to arise from her tomb and cry out to overweight, sallow-eyed doubters, "Come, see a man who told me everything I ever did" (John 4:29). That's all it takes for Jesus himself to make an appearance and say, "If you have faith as small as a mustard seed . . . nothing will be impossible for you" (Matt. 17:20).

16

Building a Living Army in a Valley of Dry Bones

Would you like to leave the rat race of denominational dyspepsia? Then get started for Emmaus, that peaceful town just seven miles distant. But the town doesn't matter. It's the journey that's important. Why? Because you never know who you're going to meet on the road. Those who travel it frequently know the pleasure of having company. "Oh, look! There are other travelers! Can you see them?" Quicken your pace and pull alongside. Somewhere up ahead the bread will be broken by nail-scarred hands. And you will be lost in adoration. You will because of your appetite for God. Journey not toward Emmaus but the center of your soul.[1]

There is no more graphic parable of vitality or death than what Ezekiel gives us when the Lord sets him down in a valley of dry bones.

He led me back and forth among them, and I saw a great many bones on the floor of the valley, bones that were very dry. He asked me, "Son of man, can these bones live?"

I said, "Sovereign LORD, you alone know."

He said to me, "Prophesy to these bones and say to them, 'Dry bones, hear the word of the LORD! This is what the Sovereign LORD says to these bones: I will make breath enter you, and you will come to life. I will attach tendons to you and make flesh come upon you and cover you with skin; I will put breath in you, and you will come to life. Then you will know that I am the LORD.'" (Ezekiel 37:2–6)

These are no longer the most green, young days of evangelicalism. The sweeping crusades of Billy Graham are gone. The hot winds of secular humanism have turned into the scorching blasts of the new atheism. Sunday night church is gone, and Sunday morning church is hanging on to trap-set hymns and hyperpromotionalism of a new detente. Summer Sundays are time-out from dull sermons and the low offerings of the other nine months.

Perhaps the most honest question is what God asked Ezekiel in verse 3: "Can these bones live?"

God is not dead. He is hovering over every valley of dry bones waiting for someone to ask the magic question: Can these bones live? The question is fair, and the answer is hidden deep in the heart of faith. Faith stands up tall in the confession of the faithful. But where there is no valid confession, the faith becomes dry and brittle, the sermons shallow. The faith we claim grows dry and unavailing.

> Why are the bones dry? We have a very short religious attention span:
>
> The average church goer is exposed to fifteen minutes a week of religious input in contrast to 167 hours of outside input. Fifteen minutes is not enough to give us a Christian mindset. And even that fifteen minutes, if it is a sermon, consists of three jokes and two things to think about. Evangelicals are not getting any food. You have hundreds of starved congregations and they don't even know it.
>
> Roberta Hestenes[2]

Seek Confessional Values, Rooted in the Creeds and Covenants

Baptists have long boasted that they are not a people of any creed. When this truth was their guiding cliché, Southern Baptists (and remember, I am one) all read the Bible and held to some cherished principles that we all celebrated in such confessions as the *Baptist Faith and Message* as a statement of our commonly endorsed doctrines. The lifestyle we cherish was hidden in a second document called the *Baptist Covenant*—the written credo of our commonly endorsed values. But after thirty years of quarreling over the *Baptist Faith and Message*, many of our adherents aren't adhering to either document very closely. As far as the *Baptist Covenant* goes, I haven't been to any Baptist church that has even read it in years. Still, this covenant had as part of its content a vow not to drink or sell alcohol as a beverage and a promise to move our letter of membership to a nearer Southern Baptist church if we ever changed our address.

The *Baptist Faith and Message*, on the other hand, remains the confession of the church such as there is a confession. Baptists generally nod in its direction as their own private confession, but most of them have no idea what it says. They are, however, at least as dedicated to its truth as Presbyterians are to the Westminster Confession (though Presbyterians don't generally know what their confession says either), or the Lutherans are to their confession. The fault may be that all old-line denominationalists have come to see all such confessions as tedious.

How unfortunate!

The creeds are to faith what the Constitution is to our government. They are both great clarifiers, and when all men

> The chief duty of man is to glorify God and enjoy Him forever.
> Westminster Confession

and women get the definition in mind, their purpose is defined and their community is fixed by a common understanding. So what? Then freedom begins, and everyone understands what the limits are. Then our tears have meaning and our laughter is guaranteed. Then God is not only obeyed, he may be enjoyed by the right of our creeds.

God enjoyed?

Certainly!

He may be our *cosmic* Father, but he is our Father nonetheless. What father is there who does not enjoy the company of his children and vice versa? The point is that I am for Christians keeping in touch with their heritage and identifying themselves with those truths that their traditions have always honored. But what if no one ever honors their confessions? Then the fading confessions disappear, posting a notice that those confessors, like their confessions, are in decline.

Why? Because to ignore those truths is sooner or later to forget them. To forget them, as I said in an earlier chapter, is to give Sheila the right to move from being a Baptist to being a Sheilaite. The upside of ecumenism is the togetherness we find in exalting the same body of significant truths. The downside of ecumenism is that the less you believe, the easier it is to be one with others who also don't believe very much. The greatest impediment to real togetherness is convictions. The larger the crowd, the smaller its collective content. The greatest masses hold only little truths in common.

> Freedom from need to serve political correctness, I believe, is born in what Larry Crabb calls shameful authenticity: "Spirit of God, supply the courage I need to risk shameful authenticity that only your love revealed through your people can transform into freedom. And fill me with much gratitude for being born again into your kingdom that I live as its citizen."[3]

Political Correctness and the Little Confession

Political correctness is the enemy of the creeds. The one distinguishing hallmark of the political correctness movement is this: it is not the passion of a creed that counts; it is the greatest number who agree to it. It is not the narrowness of a confession that is admirable but the necessary width of a shallow confession. Fervor divides; passivity unites. Let's look at the long-ago sayings of Jesus and examine what they have become:

> Jesus says: "I am the Way, the Truth, and the Life."
> The political corrector adds: "Confucius does too. The meaning of *Tao* is 'the way.'"

> Jesus says: "No one comes to the Father except through me."
> The political corrector adds: "and Mohammed, of course."

> Jesus says: "Go into all the world and preach the gospel to every creature."
> The political corrector adds: "except where people don't like to hear it."

> Jesus says: "Whoever believes in me will be saved."
> The political corrector adds: "unless they believe in someone else."

Here is the brunt of the PC problem: Is there enough fervor in these amended truths to save American evangelical Christianity? I think not. The reason that Christianity spread around the globe is our faith presumption that the whole world needs to confess Christ. Every person's right to be in heaven (and thus escape hell) rests on the knife's edge of that confession. Martyrs died in Rome to say Jupiter could not avail. Missionaries died in a thousand pagan religious systems to say there is no saving faith that does not begin and end in Jesus. Muslims, who are altogether exclusionists, would say only Islam matters, not Christianity. To Muslims, Christians are infidels whose eternity is preassigned in hell. They are not big on political correctness, and the stamina of their singular view is setting jihad to roll over what to them is our spongy views of Jesus. For them, we Christians have no valid cross-cultural unity.

No Concrete Creed, No Endurance

Evangelicalism is dying because we mumble our halfhearted adjustment of the New Testament to allow our mumbling adherents the right to *kinda* confess what they *sort of* believe. Whether we can regain the stamina we once held will depend on how wholeheartedly we believe and how often we confess the Apostles' Creed.

Legend says that this creed was conceived on the tenth day after Christ's ascension into heaven. According to this view, the apostles all got together after Jesus ascended and wrote this brief confession of their faith—hence the title, the Apostles' Creed. This, of course, is not true. But the creed is old, originating between the second and ninth centuries; and for the last eleven centuries, it has remained the unitive document for all believers.

It covers every part of the Christian's faith and stands against all revisionism as the imperative doctrine for every new believer. When any new convert came to faith during the past millennium, he or she confessed this same truth. It is a wonderful unitive statement, and I suppose the roll call of heaven will find millions of Christians answering "present" by reciting this creed and trusting Jesus, the hero at its center. The church must not just confess it with their lips but also with their hearts. Maybe then we will have the stamina to stand and endure.

> The Confession of the creed is the acknowledgment of God's saving mystery.
>
> Therefore thou oughtest to dispose thyself hereunto by a constant fresh renewing of thy mind, and to weigh with attentive consideration the great mystery of salvation . . . as if on this same day Christ first descending into the womb of the virgin, were become man, or hanging on the cross did this day suffer and die for the salvation of mankind.
>
> Thomas à Kempis[4]

This Is the Age to Read Once More the Lives of Christianity's Mystics and Martyrs

A word of advice: you may need to change your reading habits. Determine to read the Bible through in a brief span of time—in one year or less is a good plan. There are lots of reading guides to help you do this. Too many read only haphazardly from the Bible or read none at all. After reading all the riches of God in the Bible, read the lives of mystics and martyrs. I used to couch all my deeper-life courses in spiritual formation around a very few books. But beware. This high-octane truth will be yours only as *you give and hazard all you have.* It will form your inner life and also addict you to an ever-deepening love affair with Jesus Christ. I have never known anyone who took this great literature seriously who did not end up seeming somewhat more distant and mystical, even to themselves. But that's the risk you must run in living on the edge of great truth.

Hanging around Christian bookstores will only addict you to the lesser truths of our own poorly furnished, cable-driven, hero-worshiping world. But there exists, beyond this murky-glitzy world, people

> Now I guard no flock, nor have I any other employment: my sole occupation is love.
>
> St. John of the Cross

who died in flame and sword, who said and felt great things in their pursuit of divine love. I have fashioned an entire way of life from their dynamic adoration.

I learned commitment from Jim Elliot who, six years before he died a martyr, wrote in his journal: "He is no fool who gives what he cannot keep to gain what he cannot lose." Elisabeth Elliot, his widow, later wrote two books that changed me as a sophomore in college: *Through Gates of Splendor* and *Shadow of the Almighty.* During Amy Carmichael's struggle in India, she composed the poem "No Scar?" I not only learned but memorized those few words that I live with when I'm prone to desire success for all the wrong reasons. From A. W. Tozer I learned *The Pursuit of God*; from Mother Teresa of Calcutta I learned to hunger for *Life in the Spirit*; and from Eugene Peterson to *Run with the Horses*.

We are indeed what we read. This is an important truth. As the computer industry would teach us, the content of every soul is GIGO—garbage in, garbage out. Spiritually we are what we eat (read). And within our power to understand the world is the joy of knowing that reading is step one in sound analysis of any kind. Understanding the world is listening to the heartbeat of those who walked with God and who, in the walking, wrote their own particular definitions of faith. Our hearts are the drumbeat that summons the world. When they beat not, the world goes unsummoned and faith is drained of missionary power. The secularized church is footless and increasingly weak.

> I cannot understand how religious people are able to live satisfied without the practice of the presence of God.
>
> Brother Lawrence

But what does all this study of the saints accomplish? It acquaints you with the hungers of your life. And when you are hungry for Christ, there is a likelihood that you may seek him with all your heart.

Will this save evangelicalism?

Yes.

How?

It will save it when you are committed to the practice of your highest devotion. Then you may pause to wonder how Jesus feels about the world where he has placed you. Only when you see his love for this insignificant planet will you be properly motivated to win it for him. You cannot love him and not see his holy love and his passion for redemption. And that alone is the path back to the vitality we have lost. The church should be a community center instead of a desolate armory in a fallen world.

Finally, vitality is born by living in its own company. We must once more get in touch with a congregation in which preaching and teaching are closely tied to Scripture.

Finding a Bible-preaching church is a cliché to some extent, for it may seem that all churches do some of it. But the difference is that those who use the term overtly to describe themselves have the concept that every sermon summons the original text to a front and center position and calls on the Bible to intersect the day-to-day issues of life.

"Preach the word," wrote Paul; "be prepared in season and out of season; correct, rebuke and encourage—with great patience and careful instruction." Then the apostle seemed to write a specific word for our diminished day: "For the time will come when people will not put up with sound doctrine. Instead, to suit their own desires, they will gather around them a great number of teachers to say what their itching ears want to hear" (2 Tim. 4:2–3).

It is not a sterile word that we need; we need one that is being practiced by the preacher who brings us the Word. We need no preacher who struts in on Sunday, feeling sufficient in his love for God. We need one who is needy. Only a needy preacher will ache enough to inhabit heaven and convince us he actually is en route. Only a breaking heart can preach to broken hearts. We need a guide who is looking for the same light he extends in the darkness.

Finally, evaluate your own intentionality to be involved in missions and evangelism. I find so many references in the Bible about the necessity of winning the lost that I dare not close my eyes to them and tell myself they do not exist. They do exist! God wants all the world to call him Lord, and we must teach them that God longs for them to call on him. Thérèse of Lisieux burned with the fire of evangelism. She didn't burn with this fire because she wanted to enlarge Catholicism. She did so because she identified with the longing of her Savior. So must our longing be—not to save evangelicalism but for no other reason than it is the longing

219

I should like to wander through the world, preaching Your Name and raising Your glorious Cross in pagan lands. But it would not be enough to have only one field of mission work. I should not be satisfied unless I preached the Gospel in every quarter of the globe and even in the most remote islands. Nor should I be content to be a missionary for only a few years. I should like to have been one from the creation of the world and to continue as one till the end of time.

Thérèse of Lisieux[5]

of our Savior. To care what Jesus cares about is our most intimate step of identity with him.

In complying with Christ's command to win the lost, you will be flying in the face of all those who serve the bad news of political correctness, which will tell you that you should never try to change people's religion. It is wrong to ask anyone to change messiahs; it is better to accept them as they are. Then you will have to make a decision whether to obey Christ or political correctness. The world needs to come to Christ, and we exist to help him with his global transformation. Obey his call. Obedience is our response. To learn the art of his obedience is to hear him call to us across the final gates, "Well done, good and faithful servant; you were faithful over a few things, I will make you ruler over many things" (Matt. 25:21 NKJV).

Conclusion

Will the longing after Christ's final commendation turn the world around and reverse the dying? No; for none except yourself. But remember that any effort you start to reclaim the world begins in your heart. Reclaim first yourself and then the world. Do not lay this effort on yourself as though it is your calling to bring enlightenment to your continent. To adopt such a messiah complex will destroy your peace and leave you the victim of a dark neurosis. You are out to develop what the book of Hebrews calls *faith rest*. This state of faith rest is enjoying your salvation until you have joy in celebrating it. If you serve him too aggressively, you cannot possibly enjoy him. If you determine to enjoy him without serving him, you may talk yourself into a *God feeling*, but you will leave the world in no better shape than you found it.

The issue of peace is not to run ahead of Christ, fanatic in your attempt to impress him with how much you care. No, your peace will come in Emmaus, where you learn the walk, and your spirit is afire with his presence. And you will be like a bridegroom on his honeymoon night. You will know the fullest reaches of love. You will treasure ahead of time the years that will be lived in the anticipation of spiritual ecstasy. You will hunger to grow, for you have tasted intimacy with Christ. You will understand that the years yet to come to you are the promise of a walk in our exotic vineyard, where the wine holds a new intoxication every morning.

It is odd, isn't it, that God would begin such a worldwide movement in such a tiny place as your soul? But that is how it is. So let us begin what I believe is the only hope for the vanishing evangelical. Let us seek him where he may be found. Put no expectation on any church. The splendor is not somewhere out there. The revolution is in you! Whatever others may do in the forefront of this great flame, do only as he bids you. Then Christianity will be born in vitality in at least one place: within your own small heart. Either there or nowhere.

Notes

Preface

1. Got Questions Ministries, "What Is Evangelicalism?" http://www.gotquestions.org/evangelicalism.html.

2. George Marsden, *Reforming Fundamentalism* (Grand Rapids: Eerdmans, 1987).

3. Carl F. H. Henry, quoted in ibid., 69.

4. Henry, quoted in ibid.

5. Ibid., 4.

6. Jacques Barzun, *From Dawn to Decadence* (New York: Harper Collins, 2000), xvii.

7. Ibid, xiii.

8. Philip Jenkins, *The Next Christendom: The Coming of Global Christianity* (New York: Oxford University Press, 2002), 2.

9. Ibid.

10. Thomas Friedman, *The World Is Flat* (New York: Farrar, Strauss and Giroux, 2005), 339–40.

11. Ibid., 341.

Part 1 The Current State of an Inexplicit Gospel

1. Larry Crabb, *Real Church, Does It Exist? Can I Find It?* (Nashville: Thomas Nelson, 2009), xii–xiii.

2. Richard J. Krejcir, "Statistics and Reasons for Church Decline," Into Thy Word Ministries, www.intothyword.org/apps/articles/?articleid= 36557.

3. Scott Thumma, Ph.D., "Exploring the Megachurch Phenomena: Their Characteristics and Cultural Context," Hartford Institute for Religion Research, http://hirr.hartsem.edu/bookshelf/thumma_article2.html; based on Scott Thumma, Dave Travis, and Rick Warren, *Beyond Megachurch Myths: What We Can Learn from America's Largest Churches* (New York: Jossey-Bass, 2007).

Chapter 1 The Edge of Relevance

1. Leonard Sweet and Frank Viola, *The Jesus Manifesto: Restoring the Supremacy and Sovereignty of Christ* (Nashville: Thomas Nelson, 2010), 14.

2. Robert Bellah, Richard Madsen, William M. Sullivan, and Steven M. Tipton, *Habits of the Heart* (Los Angeles: University of California Press, 1996).

3. Ibid.

4. The United Church of God, *The Church Jesus Built*, 56. See www. ucg.org/booklet/church-jesus-built.

5. Cathy Lynn Grossman, "More Americans Tailoring Religion to Fit Their Needs," *USA Today*, September 14, 2011.

6. Brian D. McLaren and Tony Campolo, *Adventures in Missing the Point: How the Culture-Controlled Church Neutered the Church* (Grand Rapids: Zondervan, 2003), 78.

7. Dave Tomlinson, *The Post Evangelical* (Grand Rapids: Zondervan, 2003), 31.

8. Ibid.

9. Barbara Kingsolver, *The Poisonwood Bible*, quoted in Jenkins, *Next Christendom*, 41.

10. Jenkins identifies the global North as Europe, North America, and Japan and the global South as all other countries (not all of which are in the Southern Hemisphere). Jenkins, *Next Christendom*, 4.

11. "The Jesus Factor," *Frontline*, interview with Richard Cizik, vice president for governmental affairs of the National Association of

Evangelicals, November 12, 2003, www.pbs.org/wgbh/pages/frontline/shows/jesus/evangelicals/vote.html.

Chapter 2 When Big Isn't Great

1. George Barna, *The Frog in the Kettle* (Ventura, CA: Regal Books, 1990), 137.

2. Quoted from "Contemporary worship music," Wikipedia, March 12, 2013, http://en.wikipedia.org/wiki/Contemporary_worship_music.

3. Mircea Eliade was a philosopher and historian of religion who was known for his theory of *eternal return*, the ability to return to one's myths.

4. From the story of Sundar Singh, who died while taking the gospel to Tibet. DC Talk, *Jesus Freaks: Stories of Revolutionaries Who Changed Their World—Fearing God, Not Man* (Grand Rapids: Baker, 2002), 168.

5. Liberty University was founded as Lynchburg Baptist College in 1971 by Jerry Falwell.

6. Charles Colson and Harold Fickett, *The Faith Given Once for All* (Grand Rapids: Zondervan, 2008), 25.

Part 2 Believing Enough to Survive

1. Tullian Tchividijian, *Do I Know God? Finding Certainty in Life's Most Important Relationship* (Colorado Springs: Multnomah Press, 2007), 44–45.

2. David Kinnaman, *You Lost Me: Why Young Christians Are Leaving the Church . . . and Rethinking Faith* (Grand Rapids: Baker, 2011), 17.

3. Os Guinness, *Fit Bodies, Fat Minds: Why Evangelicals Don't Think and What to Do about It* (Grand Rapids: Baker, 1994), 24.

Chapter 3 A Passion of Pretense, a Worship of Disinterest

1. George Croly, "Spirit of God, Descend Upon My Heart," 1860; quoted in Mark Noll, *The Scandal of the Evangelical Mind* (Grand Rapids: Eerdmans, 1994), 144.

2. Paul Johnson, *A History of Christianity* (New York: Simon and Schuster, 1976), 517; quoted in Robert Bork, *Slouching towards Gomorrah: Modern Liberalism and American Decline* (New York: Harper Collins, 1986), 295.

3. Barna, *Futurecast*, 145.

4. Ibid.

5. Ibid.

6. The following information is taken from George Barna, *Grow Your Church from the Outside In: Understanding the Unchurched and How to Reach Them* (Ventura, CA: Regal Books, 2002). See also www.barna.org/barna-update/article/18-congregations/45-new-statistics-on-church-attendance-and-avoidance.

7. John Irving, *A Prayer for Owen Meany* (New York: Ballantine Books, 1989), 1.

8. Anne Graham Lotz, 2011; taken from the promotional information for the documentary "A Wake-up Call for God's People." See www.god.tv/node/3573.

9. Peter Kreeft, *Heaven, the Heart's Deepest Longing* (New York: Harper and Row, 1980), 84.

10. Ibid., 84–85.

11. Barna, *Futurecast*, 151.

12. Justin Martyr, *Dialogue with Trypho the Jew: The Early Christians*, ed. Eberhard Arnold (Farmington, PA: Plough, 1970), 298.

13. Josh McDowell, *Evidence That Demands a Verdict* (San Bernardino, CA: Here's Life Publishers, 1979).

14. Mike Yaconelli, quoted in Tomlinson, *Post Evangelical*, 42.

15. Barzun, *From Dawn to Decadence*, 26.

16. Ibid., 360.

17. Erich Fromm, *The Sane Society* (New York: Henry Holt, 1955), 11.

Chapter 4 Snuggling in with Culture

1. Tim LaHaye, quoted in *The Door Interviews*, ed. Mike Yaconelli (Grand Rapids: Zondervan, 1989), 177.

2. Jimmy Williams, "Marriage, Sexuality and Personal Development," revised by Jerry Solomon, Probe Ministries, www.probe.org/site/c.fdKEIMNsEoG/b.4218319/k.61C0/Why_Wait_Till_Marriage.htm.

3. Brian McLaren, *A Generous Orthodoxy* (Grand Rapids: Zondervan, 2006).

4. Marilyn Mellowes, "Thomas Jefferson and His Bible," *Frontline*, www.pbs.org/wgbh/pages/frontline/shows/religion/jesus/jefferson.html.

5. Mike Yaconelli, quoted in Tomlinson, *Post Evangelical*, 112.

6. Tomlinson, *Post Evangelical*, 69–70.

7. Ibid., 112.

8. John Stott, *Evangelical Truth: A Personal Plea for Unity, Integrity and Faithfulness* (Downers Grove, IL: InterVarsity, 1999).

Part 3 The Politics of Missons in the Global North

1. Quoted from correspondence with an anonymous source in Klaus Issler, *Living into the Life of Jesus* (Downers Grove, IL: InterVarsity, 2012), 176–77.

2. Howard A. Snyder, quoted in *Door Interviews*, ed. Yaconelli, 114–15.

3. R. C. Sproul, quoted in ibid., 261.

Chapter 5 Short-Term Missions and the Small Commission

1. Sweet and Viola, *Jesus Manifesto*, 67.

2. Barbara Brown Taylor, *An Altar in the World: A Geography of Faith* (San Francisco: Harper One, 2009), 95.

3. McLaren and Campolo, *Adventures in Missing the Point*, 11.

4. Jenkins, *New Christendom*, 40.

5. James Michener, *Hawaii* (New York: Fawcett, 1986).

6. Mother Teresa of Calcutta, *Life in the Spirit* (New York: Harper and Row, 1983), 1.

7. Ibid., 10.

8. Erwin Raphael McManus, *An Unstoppable Force: Daring to Become the Church God Had in Mind* (Loveland, CO: Group Publishing, 2001), 20.

9. Ibid., 43.

10. Sweet and Viola, *Jesus Manifesto*, xxii.

11. See Carolina Maria de Jesus, *Child of the Dark: The Diary of Carolina Maria de Jesus*, 50th anniv. ed. (New York: Signet Classics, 2003), 11, 57.

12. Viola and Sweet, *Jesus Manifesto*, 107–8.

13. Brown Taylor, *Altar in the World*, 47.

14. Paul McKaughan, Dellanna O'Brien, and William O'Brien, *Choosing a Future for U.S. Missions* (Monrovia, CA: Marc Publishers, 1998), 10.

15. Ibid.

Chapter 6 Can a Sick Narcissism Heal a Broken World?

1. Christopher Lasch, *The Culture of Narcissism* (New York: Norton, 1979), 53.
2. Ibid., 10.
3. Barna, *Frog in the Kettle*, 29.
4. Thumma, "Exploring the Megachurch Phenomena."
5. Sweet and Viola, *Jesus Manifesto*, 20.
6. Jenkins, *Next Christendom*, 1–2.
7. John Spong, quoted in ibid, 121.
8. Jenkins, *Next Christendom*, 123.

Part 4 The Dull Information Age

1. Neil Postman, *Technopoly* (New York: Vintage, 1993), 118, 120.
2. Cathy Lynn Grossman, "Church Outreach Takes on New Technical Touch," *USA Today*, April 18, 2012, 3A.
3. Calvin Miller, "Preaching Points: Getting Intimate on the Jumbotron," *Preaching*, online magazine, www.preaching.com/resources/articles/11645835.

Chapter 7 The Flat-Earth Evangelical

1. Warren Wiersbe, *Preaching and Teaching with Imagination: The Quest for Biblical Ministry* (Wheaton: Victor Books, 1997), 73.
2. Barbara Tuchman, *The Guns of August* (New York: Presidio Press, 1962); *Stilwell and the American Experience in China, 1911–45* (New York: Macmillan, 1970); *A Distant Mirror: The Calamitous 14th Century* (New York: Ballantine, 1978).
3. Marshall McLuhan, *Oxford Dictionary of Quotations*, 208.
4. Postman, *Technopoly*, 61–62.
5. Friedman, *The World Is Flat*.
6. Marshall McLuhan, *The Gutenberg Galaxy* (Toronto: University of Toronto Press, 1962), 36.
7. Postman, *Technopoly*, 15.
8. Ibid., 115.
9. Ibid., 114.
10. Bryant Evans, "Internet Pornography," *The Preacher's Study*, May 21, 2009, http://preachersstudyblog.com/2009/05/internet-pornography.
11. Postman, *Technopoly*, 59.

Chapter 8 The Computer Age and the Loss of Intimacy and Mystery

1. Postman, *Technopoly*, 61.

2. Accusation made against Galileo by the old cardinal in Bertolt Brecht's play *Galileo* (New York: Grove Press, 1966), scene 5, 73.

3. The material in this section is taken from Calvin Miller, "Preaching Points: Getting Intimate on the Jumbotron," *Preaching*, online magazine, www.preaching.com/resources/articles/11645835.

4. Salman Rushdie, quoted in Daniel Taylor, *Creating a Spiritual Legacy: How to Share Your Stories, Values, and Wisdom* (Grand Rapids: Brazos, 2011), 73.

5. Rachael Freed, quoted in Taylor, *Creating a Spiritual Legacy*, 97.

6. Barna Newsletter, April 12, 2010.

7. Thumma, "Exploring the Megachurch Phenomena."

8. Ernest Becker, *The Denial of Death* (New York: Free Press, 1973).

Part 5 Preaching Smart in a Dumb-Down Culture

1. Vernon Grounds, "Evangelicalism and Social Responsibility," in *Tough-Minded Christianity*, ed. William Dembski and Thomas Schirrmacher (Nashville: Broadman and Holman, 2008), 43.

2. Richard Selzer, "Have Modern Doctors Lost Their Souls?" *The Wittenburg Door*, July/August, 1989, 27.

3. George Barna, *Revolution* (Wheaton: Tyndale, 2005), back jacket.

Chapter 9 Defining Ourselves

1. Issler, *Living into the Life of Jesus*, 31.

2. Nels F. S. Ferré, "Present Trends in Protestant Thought," *Religion in Life* 17 (1948): 336; quoted in Noll, *Scandal of the Evangelical Mind*, 132.

3. Barna, *Revolution*, 49.

4. Ibid.

5. Noll, *Scandal of the Evangelical Mind*, 3.

6. Harry Blamires, *The Christian Mind: How Should a Christian Think?* (London: SPCK, 1963), vii, 3; quoted in Guinness, *Fit Bodies, Fat Minds*, 11.

7. Charles Malik, quoted in Guinness, *Fit Bodies, Fat Minds*, 11.

8. Noll, *Scandal of the Evangelical Mind*, 79.

9. Guinness, *Fit Bodies, Fat Minds*, 16.

10. John Milton, quoted in Barzun, *From Dawn to Decadence*, 262.

11. Hans Rookmaaker, quoted in Nancy Pearcey, *Saving Leonardo* (Nashville: Broadman and Holman, 2010), 103.

12. David Gobel, quoted in ibid., 76.

13. Pearcey, *Saving Leonardo*, 101.

14. William Sloan Coffin, *Credo* (Louisville: Westminster John Knox, 2004), 146.

15. The "Diadem" is a favorite choir tune setting for "All Hail the Power of Jesus' Name." It was composed by James Ellor in 1838.

Chapter 10 A Plea for the Marriage of Mind and Heart

1. Noll, *Scandal of the Evangelical Mind*, 213.

2. Sloan Coffin, *Credo*, 82.

3. Pearcey, *Saving Leonardo*, 26.

4. Barna, *Revolution*, 52.

5. Ibid., 10.

6. Ibid., 64–65.

7. Pearcey, *Saving Leonardo*, 210–11.

8. Calvin Miller, *Preaching: The Art of Narrative Exposition* (Grand Rapids: Baker, 2010), 34–35.

9. Jean Danielou, "Le Symbolisme des Rites Baptismaux," *Dieu Vivant* 1 (1945): 17, quoted in Sweet and Viola, *Jesus Manifesto*, 97.

10. Daniel Taylor, *Creating a Spiritual Legacy*, 23.

11. Pearcey, *Saving Leonardo*, 77.

12. T. S. Eliot, *The Cocktail Party*, act 1, scene 4.

Part 6 The Secular Onslaught

1. Pearcey, *Saving Leonardo*, 246. Pearcey quotes from C. P. Snow, *The Two Cultures* (Cambridge: Cambridge University Press, 2012).

2. Sweet and Viola, *Jesus Manifesto*, xix.

3. Jenkins, *Next Christendom*, 94.

Chapter 11 Lions Ten, Christians Zero

1. Robin Williams, quoted in Lasch, *Culture of Narcissism*, 53.

2. Stanley Hauerwas and William Willimon, *Resident Aliens: A Provocative Christian Assessment of Culture and Ministry for People Who Know That Something Is Wrong* (Nashville: Abingdon, 1989), 17.

3. Sloane Coffin, *Credo*, 17.

4. From a sermon by Kent Spann, *Nelson's Annual Preacher's Sourcebook 2010*, ed. Kent Spann and David Wheeler (Nashville: Thomas Nelson, 2010), 218.

5. Bork, *Slouching towards Gomorrah*, 4–5.

6. Charles Krauthammer is a Pulitzer Prize–winning syndicated columnist.

7. C. S. Lewis, *The Screwtape Letters* (New York: HarperCollins, 2001), 155.

8. Willimon and Hauerwas, *Resident Aliens*, 15–16.

9. Bork, *Slouching towards Gomorrah*, 2.

10. Tomlinson, *Post Evangelical*.

11. William Wordsworth (1770–1850).

12. Friedman, *The World Is Flat*, 137.

13. Friedman, *The World Is Flat*, 137.

14. Malcolm Boyd, *Are You Running with Me, Jesus?* (Cambridge, MA: Cowley, 2006).

15. Pearcey, *Saving Leonardo*, 47.

16. Bork, *Slouching towards Gomorrah*, 124.

17. Ibid., 150.

18. Ibid.

Chapter 12 The Culture of Secular Cities

1. C. S. Lewis, *The Screwtape Letters*, 135.

2. Thomas R. Smith, "Robert Bly and the Men's Movement," www.menweb.org/blysmith.htm.

3. Patrick Morley, "The Next Christian Men's Movement," *Christianity Today*, posted September 15, 2000, www.christianitytoday.com/ct/2000/september4/6.84.html.

4. Laurie Beth Jones, *Jesus C.E.O* (New York: Hyperion, 1995), 7.

5. Ibid., 10–11.

6. Calvin Miller, *The Path of Celtic Prayer* (Downers Grove, IL: InterVarsity, 2007), 24–25.

Part 7 The Denomination Conglomeration

1. George Barna, *Frog in the Kettle*, 137.

2. "Religious Beliefs and Practices," report 2, Pew Forum on Religion and Public Life 2007.

3. George Barna Group, "Most American Christians Do Not Believe That Satan or the Holy Spirit Exist," February 2011, www.barna.org/barna-update /article/12-faithspirituality/260-most-american-christians-do-not-believe -that-satan-or-the-holy-spirit-exis.

Chapter 13 Denominational Dyspepsia

1. Paraphrase from Issler, *Living the Life of Jesus*, 179.
2. Stephen Covey, *First Things First* (New York: Free Press, 2003), 17.
3. See the 2007 Pew Religious Landscape Survey.
4. Barna, *Frog in the Kettle*, 114.
5. Ibid., 15.
6. Dinesh D'Sousa, *What's So Great about Christianity?* (Washington, DC: Regnery, 2007), 4.
7. Barna Group, "Most Twenty-Somethings Put Christianity on the Shelf Following Spiritually Active Teen Years," September 11, 2011, www.barna .org/barna-update/article/16-teensnext-gen/147-most-twentysomethings -put-christianity-on-the-shelf-following-spiritually-active-teen-years?q =twentysomethings+put+christianity+s.
8. Census Bureau report, cited in Richard Krejcir, "Statistics and Reasons for Church Decline," Into Thy Word Ministries, www.intothyword. org/apps/articles/?articleid=36557.
9. Ibid.
10. Ibid.
11. Ibid.
12. Lasch, *Culture of Narcissism*, 53.
13. Barna, *Frog in the Kettle*, 137.
14. Barna Group, "Most Twenty-Somethings Put Christianity on the Shelf."

Chapter 14 Believing Too Little Too Late

1. Jewish guide in Israel, quoted in Dottie Parish, *Changing Churches* (Enumclaw, WA: Winepress, 2012), 126.
2. Lasch, *Culture of Narcissism*, 25.
3. Ibid., 27.
4. Calvin Miller, *The Singer*, Canto Sixteen, Introductory Epigram (Downers Grove, IL: InterVarsity, 1975), 95.

5. Calvin Miller, *Spirit, Word and Story* (Nashville: Word, 1989), 189.

6. Matthew Arnold (1822–1888), "The Scholar Gypsy," stanza 18.

7. Barna Group, "Most Twenty-Somethings Put Christianity on the Shelf."

8. Ibid.

9. D'Sousa, *What's So Great*, 4.

10. Jonathan Merritt, "What's in a Name," Op Ed, *USA Today*, September 26, 2011.

11. Ibid.

12. Ibid.

Part 8 A Recovery of Passion and Discipline

1. Kinnaman, *You Lost Me*, 57–58, 202.

2. Ibid., 22.

Chapter 15 The Search for Passion and Discipline

1. Julian of Norwich, *Showings*, trans. James Walsh (Mahwah, NJ: Paulist Press, 1978), 187–89; quoted in Calvin Miller, *Walking with the Saints: Through the Best and Worst Times of Our Lives* (Nashville: Thomas Nelson, 1995), 107.

2. Barna, *Futurecast*, ix.

3. St. John of the Cross, quoted in Robert Llewelyn, *The Joy of the Saints* (Springfield, IL: Templegate, 1988), 45.

4. George Orwell, quoted in *Nelson's Annual Preacher's Sourcebook*, ed. Spann and Wheeler, 318.

5. J. B. Phillips, *Your God Is Too Small* (New York: Macmillan, 1961), 122–23.

6. Ibid., 122.

7. Ibid., 122–23.

8. Miller, *Walking with the Saints*, 108–9.

9. Barack Obama, quoted in *Nelson's Annual Preacher's Sourcebook*, ed. Spann and Wheeler, 219.

10. William Cowper, quoted in Miller, *Walking with the Saints*, 28.

11. Madame Guyon, quoted in ibid., 220.

12. Thomas à Kempis, *The Imitation of Christ*.

13. Ibid.

14. Randy Alcorn, *Heaven* (Wheaton: Tyndale, 2004).

Chapter 16 Building a Living Army in a Valley of Dry Bones

1. Miller, *Walking with the Saints*, 236.
2. Roberta Hestenes, quoted in *Door Interviews*, ed. Yaconelli, 238.
3. Crabb, *Real Church*, 44.
4. Thomas à Kempis, *The Imitation of Christ*.
5. Thérèse of Lisieux, from her autobiography, *The Story of the Soul* (New York: Random House, 2001), 160.

Calvin Miller (1936–2012) served as a pastor for over thirty years and was also research professor and distinguished writer in residence at Beeson Divinity School in Birmingham, Alabama. He was a beloved author of more than seventy books of popular theology and inspiration, including *Preaching: The Art of Narrative Exposition.*

Also Available from
CALVIN MILLER

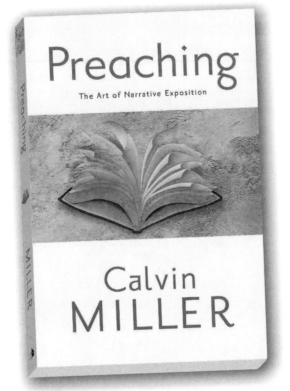

"A lifetime of preaching and teaching the art of preaching crackles and pops in this bonfire of a book. Calvin Miller, one of our best preachers and writers, tells us what he does best—and why and how."

—EUGENE PETERSON, professor emeritus of spiritual theology, Regent College